Using Social Media in Libraries

Best Practices

Edited by
Charles Harmon
Michael Messina

THE SCARECROW PRESS, INC.
Lanham • Toronto • Plymouth, UK
2013

Published by Scarecrow Press, Inc.
A wholly owned subsidiary of The Rowman & Littlefield Publishing Group, Inc.
4501 Forbes Boulevard, Suite 200, Lanham, Maryland 20706
www.rowman.com

10 Thornbury Road, Plymouth PL6 7PP, United Kingdom

British Library Cataloguing in Publication Information Available

Library of Congress Cataloging-in-Publication Data

Using social media in libraries : best practices / edited by Charles Harmon,
Michael Messina.
    pages cm
  Includes bibliographical references and index.
  ISBN 978-0-8108-8754-1 (pbk.) — ISBN 978-0-8108-8755-8 (ebook) 1. Online
social networks—Library applications. 2. Social media. 3. Libraries and community.
I. Harmon, Charles, 1960- editor of compilation. II. Messina, Michael, editor of
compilation.
  Z674.75.S63U85 2013
  025.04—dc23

                                                                    2012044728

∞™ The paper used in this publication meets the minimum requirements of American
National Standard for Information Sciences—Permanence of Paper for Printed Library
Materials, ANSI/NISO Z39.48-1992. Printed in the United States of America

Contents

Foreword

LAURA SOLOMON
The Ohio Public Library Information Network

If your library is on Twitter, chances are good that I have unfollowed it.

Perhaps your library was the one that spammed me with multiple program announcements, first thing every weekday morning. Maybe your library posted links to an online photo album, with no context other than "Here's some photos." Possibly, your library commanded me to do things like "check it out." More than likely, your library was one of the many that simply put out boring, irrelevant tweets on a regular basis.

Most libraries fall short of my expectations on Facebook as well: yet more broadcasts of program announcements that fail to make themselves relevant to virtually anyone; walls that remain empty of content, except for the occasional bookmobile schedule; instances where the library doesn't even respond to commentary, and one is left to wonder if the library monitors the account at all. I might still "like" your library on Facebook, but I can guarantee that I am not reading its posts. Quite honestly, I'd bet that lots of other people probably aren't, either.

One of my favorite quotes about social media is from Avinash Kaushik, an analytics evangelist for Google. He says, "Social media is like teen sex. Everyone wants to do it. No one actually knows how. When finally done, there is surprise it's not better." When I show this quote to workshop audiences, they inevitably giggle; then, the laughter is usually followed by a thoughtful silence as they realize the truth of what Kaushik said. Most libraries have jumped on the oversold bandwagon that social media has become, bringing vaguely defined ideas and usually no clue about what should happen once they've arrived. The reality of doing social media work rarely compares to the hype and hopes with which libraries begin.

Social media can be a Trojan horse for libraries. It has the allure of seeming simplicity, the hype of popularity, and the element of having little or no cost. Many libraries willingly begin using social media, only to discover that there truly is no such thing as a free lunch: The ease of use doesn't compensate for having to learn the hidden rules for an organization attempting to engage patrons online. The novelty of social media can quickly wear off, leaving library staff unpleasantly surprised by the reality of actually managing one or more social networking accounts for their libraries. The task that initially seemed "fun" can rapidly become a time sink, and dealing with the occasional cranky patron in a public forum can leave staff feeling even more worn.

To make matters even more complex, using social media is much akin to building on a foundation of sand. Many librarians put a great deal of effort into MySpace, only to see millions abandon that network and move to Facebook. New networks come into being constantly, and it's seemingly difficult for many libraries to stop and evaluate before chasing the next, newest thing. Some libraries have created accounts on every major social network, hoping that one will somehow be the right one with which to engage their patrons. As soon as a new social tool hits the mainstream, a large number of libraries seem to hope that the extensive publicity associated with the new network will carry over to their own use of it.

An additional concern is that many libraries have not defined social media success for themselves. Most libraries haven't set any goals for their use of social media, other than ambiguous phrases such as "awareness of the library." This is problematic when nearly every librarian is stretched to the limit, trying to do more things in less time. Effective social media work is time intensive. For libraries to be effective in the social media sphere, they have to have clear goals and definitive ways to measure progress. Otherwise, precious staff time is wasted.

The pitfalls of social media are plentiful, but there are prizes to be won. Social media presents libraries with unequaled opportunities to reach out to patrons. In turn, it also gives those same opportunities to patrons—to reach out and engage directly with their libraries. This can be unnerving, especially to library staff that are unused to the many facets of Internet culture. Yet, it is this very two-way interchange that makes social media so exciting and full of possibilities. No other medium gives us such a direct way to get feedback and responses from our patrons, outside of face-to-face contact. It is vital that libraries not squander this chance to create stronger connections with their patrons.

Sometimes, when we work to create those connections, there can be obstacles. When I talk to librarians about using social media, one of the most common questions I get is "What happens if we get a negative comment?"

Even though I've probably fielded this question dozens of times, I'm still bewildered by it. Don't we hear negative comments in the library? How many times have we heard patrons grumble and complain? Of the hundreds of librarians I follow on Twitter, I'd lay money down on the fact that at least half or more of them have tweeted about complaining patrons. People being unhappy with the library is hardly a new phenomenon. Why should we believe that online interactions will somehow be different? It's still human beings making the comments; it's only the medium that has changed. Online interaction is still human interaction. Those staff that are comfortable dealing with unhappy patrons offline will likely be competent to do it online.

Librarians and libraries have so much to offer their online patrons—way more than mere programming announcements. Social media forces libraries to act as if they exist as an individual, rather than as an institution. This is actually ideal because it encourages our libraries to use a more human voice. When patrons connect to us online, they often want to know more about the unique facets of our organization and the people who make them up. People might see the same staff at their library all the time, but how much do they know about those individuals? How much do our patrons know about what goes on behind the scenes? Libraries can convey this kind of information and much more with social media. Is it possible for an institution to have a collective sense of humor? Or to be entertaining? Absolutely. Libraries are so much more than story times and answered reference questions: They are made up of incredible, resourceful people who want to serve the library's users. Social media gives us so many ways to highlight what makes libraries special. Sharing more about ourselves enables us to not only be more transparent to our patrons but forge stronger bonds with them as well.

Social media, when done well, is much more about relationship building than it is about promoting anything. It is this concept that is perhaps the hardest to grasp: It is so much easier to simply pull out the proverbial bullhorn and shout constantly about programs and services than to craft messages and campaigns that intrigue and interest online fans. But, to do well in social media, libraries must change how they view it. Social media is much more than just another advertising medium, and only using it this way will often cause followers to eventually tune out such messages and even disconnect entirely. Ultimately, this is the most important lesson that libraries must learn.

Despite my cynicism, there are libraries out there doing social media right. Libraries have spent significant time to compose interesting campaigns and fine-tune their social media work so it is appealing to fans and followers. Many of these libraries have put effort into planning and measuring, and they know where they're going and how they can get there. Along the way, they are picking up followers and conversing directly with them. These libraries are not frightened by the incidental bad apple in their online communities, and they recognize the value that can be had from engaging openly with them. Quite often, these libraries make social media work look easy and fun, despite the tremendous amount of energy they put into it.

In the following chapters, you'll be introduced to libraries that don't disappoint in social media. Take the time to learn how they have approached online exchanges and posting to the mutual benefit of both their patrons and themselves. Especially, work to discover how they have gotten beyond the promotional aspects of social media to make relationships with their patrons more meaningful. Once you've mastered this, chances are, I might start following your library again.

Introduction

WALT CRAWFORD
Author of *Successful Social Networking in Public Libraries*

Every library is part of a community. That's as true for Lake Minchumina Community Library in Alaska (with a community of 13) as it is for Los Angeles Public Library in California (with a community of 4 million). It's as true for the Library of Congress as it is for the smallest special library.

There's a corollary that's always been true but is now more evident than ever: Every library should converse with its community—there should be ongoing, multiway communication among the library, its patrons, and its supporters. The community needs to know what the library's doing and why. The library needs to know how it can serve the community most effectively. The library and community both need to understand changing times and changing needs.

But there's another issue here. One reason why America's public library system is the most robust in the world is sheer diversity and locality—the fact that public libraries are distinctly local institutions. "America's public library system" is almost a misnomer: The libraries cooperate but can scarcely be labeled a single system. Nor should they: One great public library could not serve local needs as effectively as America's 9,200-odd local public libraries.

I think the same is true for academic and other libraries. There's no single template for a successful special library—no reason to believe that a virtual library with embedded librarians will work as well for a law firm as it does for a technology company. There's certainly no template for academic libraries: Even the libraries of the Association of Research Libraries are wildly diverse, to say nothing of the 3,500 or so smaller academic libraries in the United States. I doubt that you could even make a case for consistency among school libraries.

Each library is distinct. Each community is different. Each set of conversations will be different and lead in slightly different directions.

SOCIAL MEDIA AND THE LIBRARY COMMUNITY

I have mixed feelings about "social media" as a term and concept: I think of social networks and online publishing as two distinct areas. But I'm in the minority, and grouping the two makes sense for this book, so I'll use the term here.

Libraries and librarians have been using social media for nearly as long as there has been social media. That's scarcely surprising: Libraries and librarians have long been early adopters, especially for technologies that are affordable.

Librarian blogs date back to at least 1998, as do academic library blogs. Public library blogs date back at least to 2000. Dozens and probably hundreds of libraries were on Facebook as soon as it was feasible—and before Facebook pages made institutional presences really workable. That continues with newer options: Libraries began using Google+ early on, and the same is true for Twitter and most other services.

Thousands of libraries now use Facebook. I'm certain that hundreds (if not thousands) have used MySpace and some still do. There are almost certainly more than 1,000 libraries using Twitter. (More than 800 library people are on Friendfeed in a single library-oriented group, the Library Society of the World, a remarkable number given Friendfeed's relatively small user population.)

Libraries on social networks reach into their communities, talking to patrons where they spend their time and ideally carrying out actual conversations, not just tossing out announcements. Both strategies—publishing and conversing—appear to work well for some libraries. Conversational approaches work especially well for smaller libraries, where patrons may know the people by name.

Online publishing doesn't reach out in quite the same manner, except to the extent that patrons add RSS feeds or other intake mechanisms to the places where they spend their time. Online publishing can yield great conversations and serve libraries well, but it's a somewhat different kind of outreach than social networks. (The lines always get fuzzy, as blog posts can result in automatic social network entries.)

AVOIDING THE SHINY WHILE RECOGNIZING CHANGE

Many libraries use social media successfully—but that's not an automatic assumption. "Build it and they will come" misquotes the movie and doesn't represent reality. There are doubtlessly hundreds of cases where librarians have wasted time and energy on social media, whether through lack of planning, choosing the wrong outlet, or failing to understand the needs of the local community.

For a while, there was a movement of sorts that encouraged libraries—all libraries, seemingly—to jump headfirst into every new social network and online publishing method. That never made much sense. What I've said of blogs is probably true for most other social media: They can be useful for almost any library, but they're not going to be worthwhile for every library.

One issue is what I call "avoiding the shiny": not adopting new social media just because they are new. Starting a Pinterest presence for your library may be a great idea if your community is receptive to Pinterest, if you have people who know what they want to do with it, and if you're reasonably certain that you can connect to the community. But starting a Pinterest presence because it's the hot new tool and you've heard how great it is for libraries— that's falling for the shiny.

How many libraries have spent significant amounts of time, energy, and possibly even money building Second Life presences when it was hot stuff? How many are still there—and find that they're reaching more than a handful of people within their own communities? Second Life was the subject of more conference programs than I can remember, with extravagant praise for this sure-fire wave of the future. It was the shiny . . . and then it wasn't. MySpace—except for the music community and maybe some other communities—has similarly gone from the shiny to, well, a second-rate social network. Was your North American library on Orkut? Is it now?

Things do change. New social networks will emerge, and ways that libraries can effectively (and properly) use such networks and online media will continue to change. In very few cases does change happen so rapidly and universally that your library needs to respond right now, without looking at the situation and planning its presence.

For that matter, even as every library is different, so is every community. As I write this, it's probably true that Facebook has users in nearly every community. I'm less convinced that every community has a large number of users who want their library to be on Facebook and will interact with it there. That may be true in most places; it may not be true in all. Once you get past Facebook, the odds of reaching the people in your community drop fairly rapidly.

Don't stop looking for new possibilities. Do try to see what your community actually uses—and where they'd most likely want the library to be.

And, of course, do check your library's existing social media activities from time to time: Are they still serving the library and the community? If not, should they be refreshed or abandoned?

SUCCESSFUL SOCIAL NETWORKING IN PUBLIC LIBRARIES

I've tended to be a late personal adopter for social networks and social media in general—I didn't start a blog until April 2005, for example. But I've been interested in how librarians and libraries actually use social media—as opposed to claims for such use—for quite a while. So, for example, I've done a number of studies of blogging by librarians and by libraries, published either in *Cites & Insights*, my e-journal at http://citesandinsights.info, or in self-published books.

Most recently, I looked at the use of Facebook and Twitter in 38 of the 50 states in fall 2011—looking at each library system and independent library to see whether it was using one or both networks and, if so, how it was using them and how well it was reaching people. The results of that study, with hundreds of examples and commentary on the situation, are published by ALA Editions as *Successful Social Networking in Public Libraries*. I recommend the book, naturally: It shows the overall scene in some detail.

FROM THE OVERALL PICTURE TO INDIVIDUAL CASE STUDIES

Successful Social Networking in Public Libraries shows the overall picture for public libraries on Twitter and Facebook but strictly from an external perspective.

This book is broader and narrower but also deeper. It offers commentaries by librarians from public, academic, special, and governmental libraries on how their own libraries have taken advantage of social media tools. That set of examples should be useful background as you consider your library's use of online publishing and social networks.

Many libraries use social media well. Many could use it better. The tools to touch your community in a variety of ways have never been so widely used, so available, and so inexpensive. Your library should be at the heart of your community. Effective use of social networks and online publishing can put you in closer touch with that community and make your library more effective.

1

Blogging for Readers

ROBIN HASTINGS
Missouri River Regional Library

As both a fun activity for library staff and a way to get a database of readers' advisory matchups that is specific to the participating public library, the state of Missouri has a "Reading Challenge" (http://mobookchallenge.blogspot .com), which is open to each library in the state. The general challenge is to read the most books over the course of a year, as a staff. The benefit to doing this—besides the fun of discovering what your coworkers are reading and getting some new book suggestions—is that the staff now have a readers' advisory database of sorts, right there at their fingertips—all coming from readers at the library. When a patron says that he or she liked a particular book, we can see if that book was reviewed by staff and, if so, what other books that person enjoyed as well. Those books can form the basis of our recommendations to our patrons.

Not only did the library get to create an extensive readers' advisory database over the course of the year, but the staff also got to compete against one another and other libraries while doing something that most librarians do naturally—read. There are statewide challenges that involve number of books read per month and pages read per month, and each library can do internal challenges as well. The Missouri River Regional Library (MRRL) chose internal challenges for the staff team (the River Readers), which consisted of the following:

- Read a book a month on a particular theme (e.g., in February, read a romance; in March, read a story by a female author).
- Upload the most posts (monthly).
- Read the most pages (by the end of the year).
- Read 500 books by July.

With these challenges in mind, I was asked to create a blog that would be easy for staff to use while giving the people running the program—Claudia Schoonover and Angie Bayne—a way to keep track of statistics and met goals.

We first met about this program in January 2012 and decided to do it immediately. The WordPress blog was set up and ready to go within a week, and the first reviews were posted on January 15. The official blog launch was done that next week on the library's main blog—by then, we had 10 reviews already posted, and reviews were being added at the rate of 3 or 4 a day. Some of the books first posted were read earlier than the date they were actually posted, so the "date read" ranges from January 2, 2012, all the way through the year.

THE BLOG

We chose a WordPress blog because of the staff's familiarity with the platform, both as users and as developers. We had a WordPress blog before we switched to Drupal 7 as our content management system for our library, and several staff had experience in posting to and managing the blogs for the library. I, as the developer, also had extensive experience with WordPress both personally and professionally and knew that it would fulfill all the requirements laid out in our first River Readers meeting. Because of the ease of customization that WordPress affords, it was our first choice. MRRL uses Drupal as the content management system for both internal and external websites, but the learning curve on Drupal is so much steeper that WordPress was chosen instead.

The blog itself would consist of multiple authors logging in as a single entity. All blog posts are posted from the MRRL staff account, rather than from individual accounts, again for ease of use by the staff and the developer of the blog—remembering a single password was easier for me to support, and I could easily help someone who was having trouble logging in because there were only two log-ins—the admin log-in and the MRRL staff log-in. This did give staff members the ability to edit one another's posts, though, so this solution to our password issues might not work for everyone.

Each reader, after logging in as MRRL staff, started a new post and began the review (Figure 1.1). After filling in all the various text fields (many customized by a plug-in; described in the next section) and uploading a copy of the book's jacket image (which came from our account with Syndetics; http://www.bowker.com/en-US/products/syndetics/), the reviewer then hit the submit button, and the review went live.

This particular workflow works because our staff is small and we trust one another not to either mess with our reviews without cause or upload and post

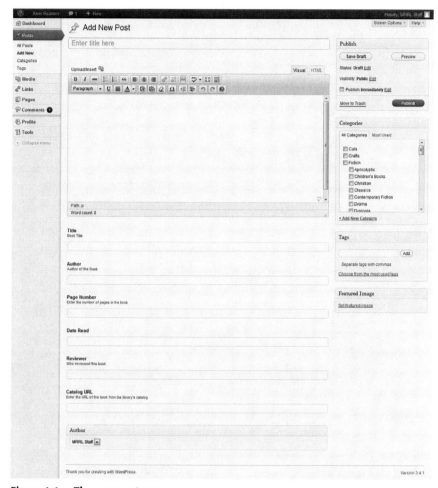

Figure 1.1. The new post page.

something really inappropriate. Again, if your staff situation is different, you can give each reviewer his or her own log-in and make each an author (one of WordPress's built-in roles), with no ability to edit anyone else's work; then, if necessary, you can set authors to require approval before the post goes live. These kinds of flexible options make WordPress a great choice for this multiuser blog.

What we wanted from the blog was the ability to make certain bits of information about the book and the reviewer modular so that it could be used in many different ways in the blog. One of the custom fields that I implemented was the "date read" field. Breaking out that information into a separate field that could be manipulated in a couple of ways was a huge help to the Reading Challenge blog team. We wanted the ability to sort and manipulate the information that staff were putting in, as well as to display that information in customized ways. To do all of this, I made use of one particular plug-in extensively.

THE PLUG-IN

The only plug-ins used on the Reading Challenge blog site are the Aksimet (http://akismet.com) spam-fighting plug-in that I add to every WordPress blog I start and the Advanced Custom Fields (ACF; http://www.advanced customfields.com) plug-in. This latter plug-in is what gave me the power to really customize the blog to do what I wanted it to do. I could create fields that were then added to the "new post" page. The fields that I added to the standard WordPress fields were

- Title
- Author
- Page number (number of pages in the book—some of our challenges involved number of pages read in a particular amount of time)
- Date read
- Reviewer
- Catalog URL (the URL of the book in our catalog so that I could create direct links to the book on each post)

The plug-in interface makes creating new fields very easy (Figure 1.2). You can add fields as you need them with little fuss. Each field added also has a number of options that let me make sure that the data being entered by the staff are what we wanted. For that "date read" field, I set it as a date field, which automatically created a pop-up calendar on the "new post" page whenever the author put the cursor in that field. There is no doubt about how the date should be entered (text, "Feb 3, 2012"; numerically, "2/3/12"; or whatever style of numeric format, "2/3/2012"), and the dates are all standardized in the database, making use of them in future pages considerably easier than if they were all added in whatever format the author chose at the time.

THE CUSTOMIZATIONS

Once you have the plug-in in place, you have access to the fields via code, too. The plug-in page has many examples of how you can access the code

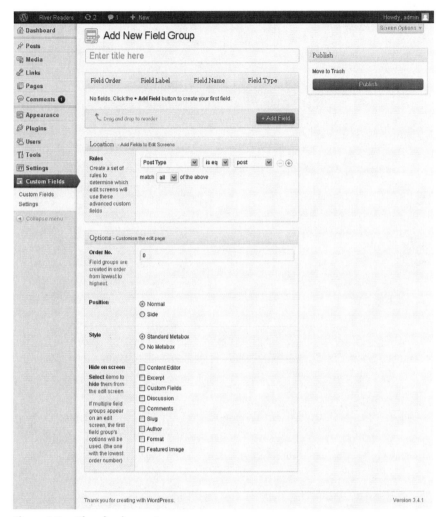

Figure 1.2.   The plug-in create page.

yourself (http://www.advancedcustomfields.com/docs/code-examples/). You can also take those examples and modify them (if you have some PHP talent in your library) to get the custom fields to display as you would like.

The big thing that Angie Bayne, our children's department manager and volunteer statistician of the Reading Challenge at MRRL, wanted was a way to see what books were read in what month in a quick glance. To do this, I created a new page on the WordPress blog and, using the code examples from the ACF page, made a query to the WordPress database that pulled all of the posts in reverse-date-read order and printed them to the page in order. The

Book	Date Read	# of Pages	Reviewer
Behind Sad Eyes	08/11/2012	235	Tracy
The First Mountain Man	08/10/2012	368	Tracy
Daughters of the Witching Hill	08/08/2012	333	Tracy
Astro Boy	08/07/2012	424	Courtney
Life as I Blow It	08/06/2012	256	Brian
Masque of the Red Death	08/05/2012	319	Angie
Dormia	08/04/2012	528	Angie
Cosmic	08/03/2012	256	Angie
The True Meaning of Smekday	08/03/2012	423	Angie
A Northern Light	08/05/2012	396	Andrea
Advent	08/05/2012	450	Tracy
Star Wars	08/03/2012	220	Tracy
Celebrity in Death	08/01/2012	389	Angie
Uglies: Shay's Story	08/01/2012	208	Courtney
Code Name Verity	07/31/2012	343	Courtney
Crossed (Matched #2)	07/30/2012	367	Andrea
Fifty Shades of Grey	07/12/2012	528	Nikki
Why We Broke Up	07/26/2012	354	Courtney
Black Dawn	07/26/2012	370	Tammy
Crusoe: Daniel Defoe, Robert Knox and the Creation of a Myth	07/29/2012	338	Tammy
The Golden Hat: Talking Back to Autism	07/30/2012	286	Tammy
A Why Spencer Perceval Had to Die: The Assassination of a British Prime Minister	07/28/2012	296	Tammy
Unbroken: A World War II Story of Survival, Resilience and Redemption	07/29/2012	473	Tammy
On an Irish Island	07/28/2012	320	Tammy

Figure 1.3.   The "books by month" list.

"books read by date" page lists the reviews with the title of the book, the date it was read, the number of pages it contained, and the name of the reviewer, in an easy-to-read table format.

   This gives Angie both the number of books read in a particular month and the number of pages those books contained so that she can create the statistics that get posted to the official Missouri Reading Challenge blog and sent out via e-mail to all staff, letting them know how the reading team is doing (see Figure 1.3).

   The query to get the information from the WordPress database was pretty simple—the code is all set up for use in the site. All I had to do was put a code block in that looked like:

```
$my_query = get_posts(array(
'numberposts' => -1,
'orderby' => date_read,
'order' => DESC
));
```

That code block sent a question to the WordPress database, asking it to send all the posts (*numberposts* =>-1 means "all of them") in order of the "date read" field in descending order (most recent to oldest). Displaying the page was just about as easy. After I set up the table in plain HTML, I added this code block to run through the results of the above query and print a line of the table per result:

```
if ($my_query)
{
foreach ($my_query as $post) {
$booktitle = get_field('title');
$bookpages = get_field('page_number');
$bookread = get_field('date_read');
$reviewer = get_field('reviewer');
echo "<tr><td>" . $booktitle . "</td><td>" . $bookread . "</td><td>" .
$bookpages . "</td><td>" . $reviewer . "</td></tr>";
}
}
```

That little block of code prints out the entire page at (http://www.mrrl. org/read/index.php/books-read-by-date/). The first line checks that there are results from the query. If there are, each result is put into the "post" variable, which is a native WordPress construct. Then, for each result, the variables *booktitle, bookpages, bookread*, and *reviewer* are set to the appropriate fields from the database. After that is done, the table row for that result is printed, and the process starts all over until there are no more results from the query; then, the whole thing stops.

With those few lines of code, using built-in WordPress functions and code samples and the ACF code examples, I created the page that listed just what Angie needed in only a couple of hours. More complicated pages—a page that grouped the results by month and changed the background color of the rows accordingly or a page that allowed Angie to choose to see only the month that she picked from a drop-down list—would be perfectly possible but more than what we really needed. This is the simplest page that does the job, and both of us were happy with it.

CATEGORIES

We also used a lot of categories to make the blog work the way we wanted it to—63 categories, in fact. We made the genre of the book a category under the main category types of *fiction* and *nonfiction*, and we made the reviewer a category under the main category type of *reviewer*. The hierarchical structure of our categories made it easy for us as reviewers to find the particular category we wanted to use and made it easy for staff and patrons to find books in a particular genre or by a particular reviewer. The categories were arranged something like this in the "new post" page:

Fiction
  • Romance
  • Paranormal
  • Historical
Nonfiction
  • Self-help
  • Business
  • Biography
Reviewer
  • Robin
  • Angie
  • Claudia

This meant that each book could be labeled as *fiction* or *nonfiction* and then further labeled with a more specific genre, such as *paranormal* or *romance*. All reviewers were made a subcategory of *reviewer* for ease of finding our names in the mess of 63 categories.

Tags were used, though not as extensively as categories. Categories were an imposed taxonomy, top-down, and somewhat difficult to change (it required an e-mail or call to me, asking me to add a new category—not terribly difficult but not an instant process most of the time, either). Those tags, however, make a nice tag cloud of "extra" descriptors of books reviewed in the blog.

RESOURCES

The resources required to pull this off were minimal. We had server space for our website, so we just added the free WordPress software to it. No money was needed for software or hardware. Staff time needed is pretty extensive—

while the reading that we do is off the clock, the blog posts can be written and posted on work time. Developer time, at least for the first week or two, can be extensive as well. The blog customizations, as detailed earlier, had to be determined, planned, executed, and then tested—each step of this process takes some time to accomplish.

In the case of the River Readers book challenge team, the resources used were zero dollars and a few hours of staff time a week, with the most being used at the beginning of the project. Another library—with fewer hardware, software, and developer resources—could easily have created the blog using the free WordPress or Blogspot services online, though the ability to customize would have been curtailed and the amount of work required to put together the statistics each month for submission to the Missouri Reading Challenge blog would have been considerably more.

THE RESULT

Blog Posts

Each blog post is customized so that the information about that book is clearly visible in the review. This is for both patrons and staff. I used a few of the custom fields to set up the custom info block at the top of the post. In the post pictured here, the custom info block consists of the title of the book (linked to the book's record in our catalog), the author of the book, and the reviewer. Information such as date read and number of pages was left off for simplicity's sake. The code to pull the custom fields and display them is very similar to the code listed earlier. On the single.php page in WordPress, the database query is done automatically; all I had to do was grab the custom fields that WordPress didn't know anything about:

```
$catalogurl = get_field('url');
$booktitle = get_field('title');
$bookauthor = get_field('author');
$bookreviewer = get_field('reviewer');
```

Now that I had that information stored in those variables, I could very easily place the information where I wanted it in the post page with an echo statement:

```
echo "<a href=" . $catalogurl . ">" . $booktitle . "</a> by " . $bookauthor
. ", reviewed by " . $bookreviewer . "< /br>";
```

Last Man Standing

23. February 2012 · Comments Off · Categories: Fiction, Paranormal, Robin, Romance

Last Man Standing by Cindy Gerard, reviewed by Robin

(Edit)

This is the last of the books in the Black Ops Series by Cindy Gerard. This book continues a relationship started back in a previous novel (Feel The Heat) between Stephanie and "Mean" Joe Green, one of the Black Ops team members. The book begins with Joe breaking up with Stephanie and heading off to what he feels is a suicide mission to avenge the death of his buddy (and Stephanie's brother), Bryan. Stephanie, being a romance heroine, doesn't just pine for Joe – she figures out what he's doing, heads to Africa and rescues him. The story is well-paced and exciting, the romance is sweet (with some sexy thrown in, of course) and the plot is both believable and thrilling at times. Stephanie manages to grow into the perfect partner for a guy named "Mean" Joe and Joe manages to lose a bit of the "hero" shine and lets her do some of the rescuing herself. This is a nice story with lots of heart and it was a fast and easy read.

Figure 1.4.   The single post.

That statement puts the custom info into the post and makes it very easy for patrons who are reviewing our blog to find the book in our catalog (Figure 1.4). It also makes it easy for patrons who find a review of a book that they like to see immediately who reviewed it and, if the reviewer liked it as well, to find other books reviewed by that person. All this is made possible by the use of the categories as described earlier.

Lists by Month and Challenges (Stats)

July: 69 books, 20,435 pages, and 8 readers—28 of those books were historical fiction (our July challenge book); Tammy (circulation department) won the month by reading 9 historical fiction books.

June: 66 books, 18, 671 pages, 8 readers—8 of those books were travel themed; Tracy (circulation department) won the month by reading 3 travel-themed books.

May: 69 books, 23,885 pages, 12 readers—5 of those books were animal themed; Janet (circulation department) won the month by reading 2 animal-themed books.

These statistics are the type of thing that Angie, our statistical whiz, sends out to the staff each month to let them know what is going on with their River Readers challenge team. The statistics are easy for regular reviewers to enter and for Angie to compile because we used the ACF plug-in for WordPress. There may have been other solutions that would have worked, but for our staff, the combination of WordPress's ease of use and the flexibility of the ACF plug-in made doing what we needed to do simple.

THE RESPONSE

The response from the community has been positive. Members have left comments on individual posts letting us know that they appreciate the reviews. Authors of the books we've reviewed have also stopped by to leave comments on their books, occasionally illuminating the review and answering questions the reviewer may have had. This just improves the quality of our blog and makes it even more useful to both staff and patrons.

Staff have been very positive about the new blog as well. Not only is it a useful tool for them professionally, but it's been a helpful tool for them personally as well. We are discovering what our fellow staff members' reading tastes are and who to go to for recommendations for new reads when we run low.

Because the service is so new and because we are still in the thick of competition for the year, no formal assessments have been done. You can see from the statistics, however, that the service is still going strong as of August 2012 and books are being added at the rate of two a day or more. This is slower than in January, when the enthusiasm was strongest, but it's still a very respectable showing for 8 months into the project that we are still reading, posting, and sharing on a regular basis.

Since this has been such a successful service so far, we do plan to continue it through the end of the year and, quite probably, do it again next year. It has been a fun activity for staff and a useful tool for staff and patrons.

LESSONS LEARNED

The biggest lesson learned has been that doing this Reading Challenge was fun. We enjoyed the process of challenging ourselves and our coworkers to read more, read more widely, and read more deliberately to provide the blog with reviews that will be of great help to future readers' advisory sessions at the reference desk. One thing that we might have done differently, if we had the chance, was to decide on what exactly would be needed by reviewers, statistics gatherers, readers, and the developer before opening the blog to reviewers. The interface was simple enough that little to no training was needed, though we did manage to confuse people by making fairly major changes to the blog and the posting interface after people had started posting stuff. Other than that, this project has been a resounding success for the MRRL's River Readers Missouri Reading Challenge team!

2

The United Nations Library Is Seriously Social

Angelinah C. Boniface

The Dag Hammarskjöld Library

Social media enables people and organizations to quickly and easily publish their own material as well as engage, connect, network, and share ideas and knowledge with others. Because social media creates dynamic new opportunities for communicators, enabling direct and real-time interactivity with United Nations (UN) audiences, the Dag Hammarskjöld Library welcomes and recognizes the benefits of these tools while acknowledging associated risks and challenges. We use social media to create awareness that can help staff generate creative ideas and expedite transfer and sharing of knowledge between working groups or teams. We follow and blog on thematic issues that involve the work of the UN and then alert our worldwide audience to the new resources as they become available. The themes include but are not limited to peace and security, international law, human rights, and humanitarian affairs.

BACKGROUND

The Dag Hammarskjöld Library is the information and knowledge center for the UN's work and activities. Librarians highlight resources and find information on a daily basis for clients around the world. However, this knowledge is not broadly shared. Therefore, the impact of what is often a long searching task is not maximized. Social media provides additional platforms for dissemination of information and knowledge. With the explosion of mobile devices and on-demand electronic applications, there is a great need for the library to be where its users are, allowing the library to be relevant in this day and age. A coherent approach on how we should use social media to create, share, connect, and disseminate information and knowledge and interact with our clients was proposed to maximize the library's outreach impact. The policy also addressed the issue of monitoring and managing by librarians to ensure efficiency and quality control.

The library serves, in priority, delegates, staff members, researchers, students, and the general public interested in the work of the UN. The UN is the parliament of the world; thus, the UN library is basically a parliamentary library. Its primary function is to enable the delegations, the secretariat, and other official groups of the organization to obtain, with the greatest possible speed, convenience, and economy, UN information resources and information needed in the execution of their duties. The purpose is to provide high-quality library services for use by delegates, missions, and UN staff members, as well as by specialized researchers, while enabling all libraries of the UN system to function as a user-oriented network. The UN library is to establish depository libraries worldwide for dissemination of UN information. This is a complex clientele with complex information needs, and social media tools will assist in addressing these needs.

The environment for providing research services to parliaments has changed. This becomes even more complex for the UN library since it is a diverse organization. The UN library is an environment where delegates need information in a rapid and spontaneous way. More often, agendas are set with outside control of our clients. The value that the library therefore brings is to respond to these queries within the most convenient time possible and to be able to deal with changing requests and demand. This new environment means that delegates expect the library and research services to support them in new ways and assist them to adopt new technology. The UN library is centuries beyond dusty book covers and now has a pioneering presence on social media.

STEPS WE TOOK BEFORE ADOPTING SOCIAL MEDIA TOOLS

Managing social media is time-consuming. Clearly defined goals and objectives on what role social media will play in the library are essential. For the UN library, all librarians are social media stakeholders. This is done through collaboration and assigning of roles and tasks accordingly. Identifying the goals and objectives was clearly a tedious and critical process. The goals had to be measurable, and they had to have an action plan, an achievement, and a desirable result. Our strategy and policy needed to guide social media activities without compromising the organization's image. *Consistency*, *integrity*, and *coherence* were the main words that guided the policy. The UN values social media, and it is important to add value to people's lives using social media. Before adopting a social medium, consider how the tool will affect clients—specifically, how will the content shared add value for both them and the parent organization?

The policy took a user-oriented approach. The UN library is mandated by the UN General Assembly on the "forefront of the use of information technology to meet the increasing demand for reliable information resources that support global problem-solving." The only way to make this goal a reality is to embrace new technology and adapt to the needs and expectations of our clients. Our social media activities focus on our client's information needs while balancing the needs, challenges, and role of the library. The idea is to involve our clients at all times. We listen to them in all the social platforms and provide resources as per their requirements and needs. We provide information resources at the most convenient time, and social media allows instant sharing. The UN library has a global clientele, and it has a distinct role. Its unique role is that it is the library of the world and holds the richest content in the whole world. The information resource that the UN library holds can be found in only this library and not anywhere else. The idea is to distribute this information resources as widely as possible to all those who need this information. It is our role to make this information accessible to those who need it; hence, social media provides a platform for sharing.

We created guidelines for all librarians (see http://un.libguides.com/socialmedia). They pertain to all the social media tools that the library is implementing. The most important thing about these guidelines is that there is sustainability. This allows for continuity in case one has to leave the organization. There is also information sharing among librarians pertaining to the activities that we are doing on social media.

The UN library tracks its social media use. We have adopted Google analytics, tweet counter, and HootSuite for tracking social media activities on all the tools. For Facebook, the Insights page is very useful. HootSuite brings together all these tools such that they can communicate and share easily with one another. It also allows for listening to our clients. HootSuite is an evaluation tool. We keep monthly statistics of the activities on our platforms. Measuring the impact of social media in the library is important. There is a growing consensus that it is the targeted behavioral change that should be measured and not the activity on the social media platforms.

THE UN LIBRARY'S SOCIAL MEDIA AGENDA

Communication

Communication is a key function for libraries. Communication technologies have revolutionized the way that libraries disseminate information. The new generation believes that e-mailing is dead. Thus, we need to shift to instant messaging, Facebook, or SMS—because that is where users are and because social media allows immediate real-time dialogue. As the library of the world, the UN library is indebted to provide access to information to all. Social media is providing a platform to share the work of the organization and engage and network with our clients.

The library follows RSS feeds of all UN family websites to get the most recent information on documents and recently published reports and publications. We blog on official records, supplements, meetings, major conferences, major issues, commemorations, international days, and international years. The essence is to provide resources rather than just an alert service.

Access to UN Information Resources

The library's primary function is to enable the 193 member states of the UN, the UN secretariat, nongovernmental organizations, intergovernmental organizations, researchers, students, and the general public to obtain—with the greatest possible speed, convenience, and economy—UN information needed for their daily duties. Researching for UN information can be a tedious and frustrating process. Issues arise spontaneously, and information pertaining to those events is needed. The organization has been dealing with issues dating back to 1945 and even beyond the League of Nations. Therefore, researching the history of agenda can be a tedious and challenging process. Our clients are also diverse. The other challenge in providing access to information is that delegates change. Member states bring in new diplomats as the need arises. This makes it a difficult process since sometimes our clients have only a vague idea of how the UN works. The most important thing about this is that we do the research for our clients and provide access to full-text resources of the issues, whenever available. This is making the life of our clients easier since, more often than not, they are required to quote the documents of past events in their current reports. It is our role to educate and equip delegates with tools and resources necessary for them to understand the organization. We blog, among other things, on new reports, publications, meetings, major events, and major conference and commemorations. We blog on issues that are happening currently at the UN. We provide historical information resources to issues since many a times, delegates are required to reference these documents.

Provide Education

There is a saying that in our organization: "In order to understand the UN, you need to understand its documentation." The UN library shares knowledge on UN documentation on social media. We provide training and coaching on a number of courses. We create online courses and videos on how to find UN information and post online, for those who cannot take in-house training (since it is available to delegates only in New York). This is a critical service since you are taking the library to where people are. They feel that they are part of this global community. Our clients also feel empowered. They are able to do research for themselves with the help of the online tutorials that we create and post online.

Respond to Positive/Negative Feedback

People are talking about your library on the web and in different social media channels. One of the most important tenets of customer service is to be responsive to your users' concerns or praise. Recognize them, and show that you are interested in and care about their opinions. There is no controlling what is said about your library anymore, but you can influence the message that comes across.

The UN library is seeking to improve its services across the board in line with the goals, objectives, and mission of the UN. The only way to do this is to listen to our clients and respond accordingly. Libraries need to learn that they are at the center of communication. Clients need to receive information from us so that they can pass it on. Responding to the feedback that we receive from our clients is good for not only the library but for our clients too, since we will be able to tailor our services to their needs.

Marketing/Advertising

Your library likely already markets its services or events using traditional media: fliers, bookmarks, announcements in calendars of events, newspaper ads, press releases, and so on. Social media is simply another form of media that you can use to get your message out there. Millions of people use social networks, and likely, a large percentage of the population you serve does too. The UN library has a lot of products that need to be pushed to clients. The library does training on how to effectively search for UN information. This is a unique product from the UN library for those who are not able to attend in-house training, which is mainly restricted to delegates. Social media plays a part by creating pathfinders or LibGuides and posting them on YouTube. The UN has activities that we also need to make our clients aware of. Our clients will be forced to follow us since they know that we are marketing not only books and trainings but a whole range of activities happening at the UN. This marketing is not an alert process. We market ourselves by providing information resources to the event that is going on. This is a unique service that the library offers. We do the research, find the resources about the event, and share the event, with the resources to our clients.

Understanding Users Better

Often people assume that they know their clientele. However, most of the time, I am very surprised at the things that I overhear or the questions that patrons ask. There is always something new to learn. As a reference librarian, I have learned more from my clients than I have from my colleagues. Social media allows conversations with other users, and these conversations reveal important insights. Simply talking with people allows you to get to know them better and, more important serve them better. Have conversations with patrons both in person and through social media. You will be surprised at what you learn.

The clients that I serve on a daily basis are new. Their questions are vague, and we sometimes have to figure it out what exactly they are looking for. This is made even more difficult by the fact that the UN is a unique organization and has its own way of doing things. A number of our clients do not understand how the UN works. We therefore equip them with the tools and resources necessary for them to do their work, and ultimately, they may understand the UN. For example, Figure 2.1 illustrates a conversation with one of our clients.

 Inas @InasBseiso   17 Feb
@UNLibrary was the A/11207 published? Can't find it

 UN Library @UNLibrary
@inasbseiso old document, not yet online - send us a request ow.ly/98I2U
↰ Hide conversation

2:44 PM - 17 Feb 12 via HootSuite · Details
↰ Reply 🗑 Delete ★ Favorite

 Inas @InasBseiso   17 Feb
@UNLibrary no not old it's yesterday's GA resolution 11207 on #Syria

 UN Library @UNLibrary
@inasbseiso Sorry for the confusion, did not relized you were looking for the press release of yesterday meeting ow.ly/98XED
↰ Hide conversation

6:20 PM - 17 Feb 12 via HootSuite · Details
↰ Reply 🗑 Delete ★ Favorite

Figure 2.1.   A conversation between the library and a client.

UN LIBRARY SOCIAL MEDIA PRESENCE

The library is now present on five social media platforms: Tumblr, Twitter, Facebook, YouTube, and SlideShare. It takes a lot of courage and dedication to adopt social media tools. It can be frustrating at times because of the amount of time spent to create a blog. For us, quality control is very critical. A lot of work and research goes into every blog that we create. There are challenges, but there is more to social media than mourning about the challenges.

Tumblr

We use Tumblr as our blog as well as an interactive platform where we post new resources from across the UN system, the main organs, specialized agencies, the UN secretariat, and offices all over the world. New publications, reports, meetings and conferences, special events, international commemorations, and so on are blogged, and relevant full text of resources are linked to cater to the information needs of followers.

We blog on Security Council meetings, General Assembly major meetings, commemorations, major conferences, international days, and international years. The main idea is to provide current awareness service while providing resources that can assist researchers with their information needs pertaining to a particular issue. Not only do we provide resources, but we also provide links to the relevant material, where possible. These blogs take a tremendous amount of time to do, depending on the research topic. Some issues of the UN are historical, dating to when the organization started, with some dating all the way back to the League of Nations. It is our responsibility as the library to make the user aware of all the resources relevant to the blog created.

Twitter

We launched Twitter in February 2010. The library started to use Twitter to disseminate UN Pulse entries. Not surprising, the number of monthly tweets is similar to the number of UN Pulse posts in 2010. At the end of 2010, the library account was followed by 1,500 users. In May, reference librarians decided to work more with Twitter and began to tweet not only on flagship UN publications that are posted in UN Pulse but also on other UN and non-UN reports. As a result, the account followers increased exponentially, and at the end of July, it had reached 4,000 followers.

We also started to tweet presearches in UNBISnet (aka library catalogue) on hot Security Council or other bodies' topics. However, the topics are recurring, and information posted on Twitter is short-lived. As a result, instead of putting every UNBISnet presearches over and over again, librarians started to blog resource pages in Tumblr, which can be reused anytime the agenda item recurs.

The library began producing screencasts on how to search for UN documents in September 2010. These screencasts are primarily incorporated in the library website through the development of online tutorials. While we use Twitter to post links and interact quickly and briefly with users, the character limitation prohibits content creation.

YouTube

We disseminate the screencasts on YouTube. The online tutorials on how to use UN research tools to search for UN documents and publications are important to our worldwide audience and to staff in peacekeeping missions, who have no other access to the library's training program. These videos allow staff to learn important skills in using online databases such as ODS and UNBISnet, the library's online catalogue to search for information.

Facebook

Facebook is the most used social media in the world. Sharing links to the blog on Facebook will ensure the broadest dissemination possible. Besides, Facebook is a great tool to interact with users, as it is possible for them to post questions and comments. Like Twitter, Facebook is a sharing tool for all the blogs. The library also uses Facebook to connect and interact with clients and other libraries.

The use of Tumblr, Twitter, Facebook, and YouTube is therefore complementary and will give the library the right platforms to create content, disseminate it, and interact more with its users. It will also complement the content of the website and ensure a coherent online presence by the Dag Hammarskjöld Library. Using several platforms will ensure that the efforts in developing social media network are not compromised when one is discontinued.

SlideShare

The library conducts training and workshops on UN documentation and other thematic areas, including the Security Council, the General Assembly, Economic and Social Council documentation, human rights, international law, RSS feeds, and commercial electronic resources. To outreach these presentations through social media, some have been uploaded to SlideShare, a Web 2.0 tool for education and information.

THE FUTURE

These are very exciting times. Libraries build communities. Libraries need to leverage these new technologies if they are to be relevant, while at the same time understanding the role that the library plays in society. Technology is advancing, and the environment is changing. Libraries should find strategies of remaining relevant without changing the role of the library. There will be challenges: shortages of staff, funding (since social media is not free), and fear. Libraries have come a long way, and nothing should stop us from doing what we know best: building communities.

3

Visualizing Information with Pinterest

Cynthia Dudenhoffer
Central Methodist University

Central Methodist University (CMU) is a small liberal arts college in rural Missouri, with around 1,200 students enrolled on the traditional campus and with another 1,500 or so enrolled in online and distance education courses. As our enrollment shifts from face-to-face contact with students to a virtual environment, the library is continually seeking ways to reach out to not only the on-campus faculty and students but also these nontraditional learners, in an accessible and appealing way. How can a library market collections to students who will never set foot in the brick-and-mortar library? How can we make our on-campus students and faculty aware of new acquisition? How can we present visualized information to make services such as research assistance more appealing? One of the most recent attempts to meet these goals has been through the use of the social media tool Pinterest. Pinterest allows members to "pin" items or images found on the Internet to a "pinboard," which can then be easily shared through an e-mail link or by following the creator. The boards are publicly viewable through the link, so no log-in is required, and the boards can be constantly updated. This type of tool lends itself very well to sharing information to visual learners and traditionalists alike, and it can be maintained by library staff quickly and easily. Library faculty can also use Pinterest to create "research portals," or visual representations of ideas used to kick off the research and writing process.

CHIEF AIMS AND OBJECTIVES

As the staff of Smiley Library searched for a tool to assist in the visualization of information, we set a few guidelines for the product or tool. First, we wanted a tool that could present images in an accessible way. We wanted something that could be multipurpose. We also looked for a product that was low in cost. Name recognition and popularity became a factor as well. We needed a tool that would allow us to visually display information for students performing research, that could push out information to online students, and that could be used by the students and sent to library faculty. But first and foremost, we wanted a tool that could help us effectively market our collections to the entire CMU community.

MARKETING NEW BOOKS AND VIDEOS

Like many small private colleges, CMU follows a subject area acquisitions model based on faculty allocations. In other words, to help the two library faculty collect materials relevant to the curriculum, a portion of the acquisitions budget is given to each academic division. The divisions then select materials they think are relevant, and they send these recommendations to the library director for possible purchase. The model works pretty well overall, especially since CMU has no subject area reference librarians. All purchasing is done by the library director, so these faculty recommendations are an essential part of the acquisitions process. One of the problems, though, is the fact that faculty want to know who is purchasing what and when it has been added to the collection.

In the past, after acquisitions have been added, we have used the integrated library system to generate a report of the newly added items and send it over e-mail. The report is a massive, unappealing list of titles and publication information, sorted by Library of Congress call number, so it is roughly grouped into subject areas. The list clogs in-boxes and is not highly utilized. Smiley Library marketed new books to on-campus students through the use of a "New Books" area within the library but had no other way to push or market these materials to the campus community. Likewise, our online students were receiving no information about new acquisitions to the collection. Library staff searched for a way to present this information to the relevant parties quickly and easily. Several products exist that can create these kind of reports, but we desired a product that was low in cost, that was easy to populate and share, and that created a stable URL that could be added to library marketing materials. After evaluating several products, we found Pinterest, a relatively new option. Pinterest met our selection criteria. It is a free social media service tied to a single log-in. It produces stable URLs that can be easily maintained. It required little or no training for use, since many staff, faculty, and students were already familiar with the site.

To use Pinterest, an account must be set up with an e-mail address and password, or an account can be tied to an existing Facebook account. We chose to set up the account with an existing Facebook page, since this made it easier to publicize new content. After setting up the account, we created a new pinboard titled "Smiley Library New Books." Now, as each new acquisition is cataloged, processed, and added to our new book collection, a picture can be snapped of the item, which can then be added to the pinboard (Figure 3.1). An annotation about the item can also be added. We have used annotations to attribute items to alumni authors, to tag them as the recommendations of particular faculty, to designate books in a series, to list award winners or nominees, and to make quirky comments that might appeal to our student community. Faculty can add content notes or class information to the "pins" as well. Using Pinterest in this way is especially helpful, considering our acquisitions model. The visual representation allows faculty to quickly locate their own recommendations, while seeing what other departments have selected as well. None of these options was available using the integrated library system–generated new book list.

Marketing our new books through Pinterest has implications for students as well. In fact, the majority of "followers" we have gathered for our pinboards are students. Once "followed," students will receive updates when

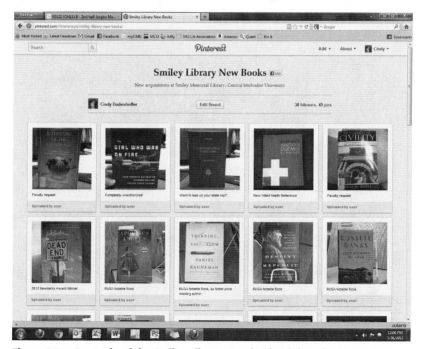

Figure 3.1.   A sample of the Smiley Library new books pinboard.

new items are added. Smiley Library's Facebook page is updated when new items are pinned, so those subscribers will see the information as well. Links to the library webpage are embedded in our course management software, so distance learning students have access to the boards whenever they log-in to courses.

CMU also maintains a popular DVD collection, funded by the student government association on campus. This collection is constantly changing, and it used very heavily by students. Student requests for new releases are constant, so the ability to quickly and easily push out available titles is a great help. Creating a new pinboard for this collection became the logical way to market the new movies and reinforce to the students that their fees were being put to good use. This additional marketing outlet cuts down on repetitive questions asked of staff, and it provides an excellent visual representation of what is in the collection. We have also annotated this collection with tags for award winners, student requests, movies used in coursework, staff recommendations, and many others. The link to the new videos pinboard is also available on the library's home page (Figure 3.2).

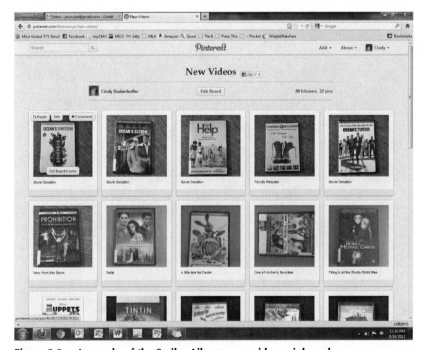

Figure 3.2.   A sample of the Smiley Library new videos pinboard.

MANAGING THE TOOL

There are many reasons why we chose Pinterest to market our collections. One of the features that adds to the value of this tool is that once a new pinboard is created, the link for that particular board remains static. In other words, we created the library's Pinterest account, then created the related boards. The URL for the board never changes, regardless of how much content is added to it. The URL can be added to the library webpage (as ours is), and it can be left alone. Members of the CMU community can add browser bookmarks for the Pinterest boards without having to update them. There is also no need for updating on the staff side: We no longer spend time running new lists or configuring PDFs of titles to e-mail out to faculty. The Pinterest site also hosts all content, so no updating is needed on that end, nor do we need server storage to hold the files. These advantages are definitely a boon for a library with limited staff.

Another advantage is that users can view the boards without creating an account. Many social media tools require users to create a basic account, providing a log-in and password, even for freely accessible versions of a tool. Pinterest boards can be viewed by anyone with access to the Internet and the URL to the boards. This fact makes the tool more appealing to faculty and nontraditional students, who are more wary of giving personal information to Internet sites.

Daily management of our Pinterest boards is a relatively simple process. Pinterest boards can be managed either through the website itself or by using the smartphone applications available for iPhones and Android products (Figure 3.3). After looking at several options, we chose to use the Pinterest iPhone app to manage content for the new book and new video pinboards. As each item is cataloged, processed, and readied for a final check before it is available for patron checkout, the technical services assistant or a work study student takes a picture of the item using the app and the smartphone's built-in camera. The picture can be cropped or altered if needed, and an annotation can be added at this point. The staff member chooses which board to add the new picture to (if multiple boards are available); then the item is automatically added to the appropriate pinboard. Initially, we utilized the website itself for adding content, searching for images of the items we were adding, and then importing them into Pinterest. However, pictures of some scholarly titles are not readily available, and the process was unwieldy. Using the smartphone application allows for pictures to be directly uploaded and annotated, therefore making it a more streamlined process. The only difficulty in using this method is that whoever is pinning the items to the board must use the iPhone associated with the library's

Figure 3.3. The Pinterest OS application.

Pinterest account, which happens to be the director's iPhone. But since our library is small and all the staff are in regular communication, this has not been a problem. The entire process of adding newly acquired items to the pinboards requires about 30 minutes a week on average for roughly 30 to 80 items. Larger libraries with a set acquisitions staff would need to examine which methods work best for their situation.

Pinterest allows for many types of "pins," so libraries not wishing to take their own pictures can pull images from Amazon or any other source that provides cover photos. When creating a Pinterest account, a "pin it" button can be added to the bookmarks toolbar in the Mozilla Firefox browser, allowing for easing pinning of book covers or other materials. Larger libraries for whom sharing a staff member's phone might not be practical will have better luck utilizing this method. The "pin it" button is also extremely useful when using Pinterest in other library applications (as discussed later; see Figure 3.4).

Though marketing these collections with Pinterest boards is new to our library, it has been well received, especially by students. The accessibility and rapid updating of the boards is popular, and as previously mentioned, we have seen a decrease in routine questions regarding what has just been added. Students were enthusiastic about the visual format and the imme-

Figure 3.4.   The Smiley Library website, with "pin it" button and links to pinboards.

diate access to new titles. As we begin new student orientation and visit students through the freshmen experience program, library staff will have more opportunities to share this new form of marketing with our students. So far, efforts to promote the library pinboards have been informal, through events such as new faculty orientations, day-to-day reference questions, and committee meetings. Smiley Library will soon be entering the next round of faculty allocations and requests, so we are hopeful that this new method of marketing and outreach will be embraced by faculty, as they will now have the ability to immediately see new additions to the collections. As of the end of August 2012, "Smiley Library New Books" has 85 followers, and the new videos board has 74 followers, which is a strong number since the boards have existed for only a little over 12 weeks, with much of this time taking place during the summer intersession. The links on the website log significant traffic as well, so the campus community is taking time to view the boards, even if those patrons do not "follow" the activity through personal Pinterest accounts. We hope to steadily increase this number; the library plans to aggressively market the boards at both library and campus orientation events in the fall semester.

PINTEREST AND INFORMATION LITERACY

Like many universities, Central Methodist has created an information literacy program embedded within beginning composition classes and writing seminars. Information literacy (or fluency, as we call it) was also included as a curricular core competency in a redesign of general education course work about 3 years ago. Since the inclusion of this competency, the library faculty, working closely with the English department, continually endeavors to make information literacy interesting and applicable to all students. Incorporating activities utilizing Pinterest have not only afforded opportunity to create engaging assignments but also provided opportunities for student to develop transliteracy skills. The activities are also easily translated into online assignments for our distance learning students, adding the extra benefit of a stable curriculum in both traditional and online settings.

RESEARCH PORTALS

At its most basic level, Pinterest is a collection of visual images. After creating an account, users collect images from across the Internet and group them under a title of their choosing. Images can be annotated with supplemental information. The idea of grouping visual information around a topic led to the creation of some unique assignments in CMU's beginning composition classes. We dubbed these assignments "Research Portals," since they serve as a jumping-off place for students to begin the research process. For example, students were asked to create a Pinterest account and then select images that related to the term *satire* (Figure 3.5). Each student is responsible for his or her own pinboard and was asked to share the permanent link to the board via the course management software. Because a term such as *satire* has a broad definition and can be interpreted differently by different people, this topic was a perfect test run for the application. Students gathered images from a huge range of sources, from Jonathan Swift to *The Colbert Report*, using the "pin it" function built into the Internet browser. Annotations were added to explain why the images were related to the term *satire*. Students were then asked to explain why they chose these images to represent satire, either as an in-class presentation or, in the online class environment, as a discussion board post. In the next step, students crafted their own definition of satire based on the images collected on both the personal board and those shared by the class. This student-generated definition then became the focus of the first assignment in a scaffolded set of papers completed throughout the semester. At the conclusion of the assignments, students were asked to revisit the pin-

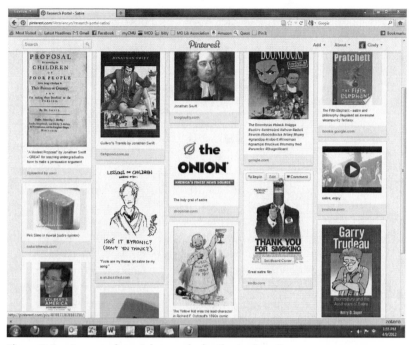

Figure 3.5. A research portal example for the topic *satire*.

boards and see if the images chosen still applied or if their perceptions had changed. Upon completion of this collection of assignments, students have developed both traditional information literacy skills, such as finding sources to support ideas, and visual literacy skills by using images to build an argument. Similar processes have been used on topics such as American culture by decade and rethinking perceptions of college life. Collecting visual images via Pinterest allows the easy juxtaposition of ideas based on what students perceive through popular culture versus what is found in reality. This juxtaposition and the ease of accessing Pinterest as a visual aid provide excellent opportunities for critical thinking and discussion. Feedback from students completing the assignments was generally positive; most found collecting images and annotating them a less daunting task than creating a traditional annotated bibliography. Most were familiar with Pinterest before using it in class, which created the helpful side effect of an increased comfort level with beginning the research process in this manner.

Smiley Library also uses Pinterest to connect students with resources in a few other ways. One is a board titled "Books Worth Reading." This pinboard is populated with books chosen by CMU faculty and staff that we believe will appeal to students. These books are annotated with short summaries and "read-a-like" information to guide students' leisure reading. We have also used the board to connect students from campus book clubs to other titles they might enjoy or subsequent books in a series. We also hope to encourage the use of Pinterest for visual bookmarking and the creation of reading lists and supplemental information for more CMU courses, since it is easily embedded into the course management system.

EDUCATIONAL TECHNOLOGY

Pinterest is also being utilized in the campus educational technology course. This course is designed to introduce future teachers and education majors to a range of technological options that can be used in the K–12 classroom. Taught as a hybrid online/traditional course, students must use technology independently to create lesson plans in their subject area. There is a focus on using tools that are freely available and require no download or hosting, since many public schools lack the resources to manage complex or costly software. Students are not only responsible for incorporating technology but also asked to consider different kinds of learners and learning styles (visual, auditory, etc.). In one assignment, students were asked to create a fully formed lesson plan that would appeal to visual learners. The content could be for any age group and any subject area, but it had to have a strong visual element and incorporate technology in a meaningful way. Pinterest has a strong appeal for visual learners, and several students chose it as the curricular tool for this assignment. For instance, a history education major created a pinboard of generals active during the American Civil War. Portraits of generals, as well as battle maps and images of troop locations, were included in the pinboard, illustrating the impact that each general had on the war. Another student in the course focused on elementary students and taught a lesson on ethnic foods. This lesson asked the students to create a "food passport" (Figure 3.6): Images of dishes and recipes from all over the world were collected via the pinboard. Students earned "stamps" in their passports by finding dishes from a variety of countries or by trying dishes from different regions, which exposed them to diverse cultures. Students were then asked to think critically about why the food cultures of these countries differed so wildly from place to place. The visual nature of Pinterest and the ease with which images can be found and freely shared make it an excellent tool for this kind of assignment. In previous iterations of this assignment, students printed images and assembled poster boards or displayed sets of images via PowerPoint. Now, our potential K–12 teachers can save and share URLs safely with future students, since no log-in is

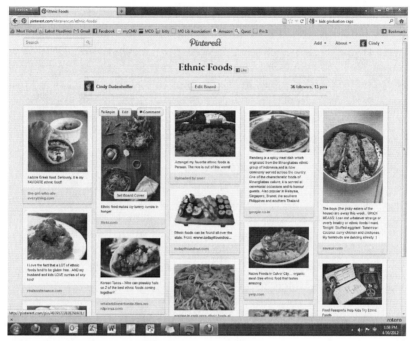

Figure 3.6. Educational technology "food passport."

required to access the boards. Pinterest allows students to capture images digitally, share them easily, and retain materials for future use.

Pinterest is thus promoted to the education majors on campus as a resource to gather ideas for future classrooms. The site has a specific area dedicated to education, which contains a huge variety of boards with everything from syllabi to ideas for classroom decorations to reading lists and resource guides. Pinterest is also completely collaborative, which makes it a great tool for group projects, especially with distance learning students located in disparate locations. Group members can share a board and pin items to it from anywhere, so creating a poster or presentation online is a simple task.

COPYRIGHT ISSUES AND THE FUTURE

The library staff at CMU knows that it can be a risky move to integrate social media into services or curriculum. Since these tools and sites change so rapidly and popularity can wax and wane, it can be difficult to create stable activities based on social media. Pinterest has also been attacked by artists and photographers worried that the image-sharing site violates

copyright laws. Pinterest recently changed its terms of service and acceptable use policies to address some of these issues. Cold Brew Labs (2012),
the company that owns Pinterest released a statement affirming, "Our goal
at Pinterest is to help people discover the things they love. Driving traffic to original content sources is fundamental to that goal" (Tsukayama,
2012). Starting June 2012, Pinterest began adding automatic citations and
credits to items pinned from popular sites such as Etsy, SlideShare, Flikr,
and Kickstarter. These citations cannot be edited by end users. In February
2012, Pinterest provided code to artists who wish to "opt out" of the pinning
process. Adding the provided code to a website will block the ability to pin
images contained on the site (Kessler, 2012). While the future of Pinterest
might be somewhat uncertain, perhaps the problems that the site is facing
can be used as yet other teachable moment: "Class, let's discuss the ethical
use of information and images found on the Internet." The concerns over
copyright did not hinder use of Pinterest in the library or in classroom settings at Central Methodist, but it did provide the opportunity for discussion.
This issue, along with information about creative commons licensing and
the proper way to credit or cite Internet sources and images, is now included
in the curriculum of our educational technology course. Likewise, copyright
issues are a component of the information fluency competency.

CONCLUSION

While Pinterest has been a part of coursework and marketing at CMU for
only one semester, students and faculty were quick to embrace its use. The
number of followers viewing the library pinboards has already outpaced usage of the text-based lists. Students in educational technology used Pinterest
to put a new spin on a visual literacy assignment. After a successful test run
in one course, the library staff hopes to further integrate the use of Pinterest
into information literacy activities, building on the satire assignments used
this year. Assessment of these activities is merely anecdotal at this time, but
students at CMU take part in a formalized information literacy test, Project
SAILS, so we will have concrete assessment data to analyze after the fall
2012 semester. The library pinboards will be included in orientation activities
for new students in the fall semester, which should drive even more traffic to
the boards and create a new cohort of students that recognize Pinterest as the
prime location for new materials.

   The next steps for incorporating Pinterest into library services include
adding cataloging information to the boards for new books and new videos.
Currently, the campus community can access the visual images of library

items, but it must then access the library's catalog separately. It is our hope to incorporate the catalog links directly into the annotations for titles, providing our patrons one-click access to locate the materials. This step is more time intensive, so use of the Pinterest boards and staff time will be carefully monitored before this step is enacted. Our other significant plan for Pinterest will be a part of our campus book clubs. While the boards have been used informally, we hope to standardize the process and provide a community board for each book club to provide a set area to share titles, related materials, and read-alikes, as well as an opportunity for virtual participation in the book club.

Pinterest is a tool that suits the small level of acquisitions, closely connected staff, and modes of communication between the library and the campus community that we maintain at CMU. Before implementing this type of tool, a library would need to examine these factors and see if Pinterest is a good fit. The process of creating boards to market materials would quickly become a time-consuming trial if too many items are added on a regular basis. Likewise, Pinterest is an informal way to communicate with patrons; it might not fit the culture of a traditional or more formal campus. I would encourage libraries interested in this tool to examine their needs with a critical eye before committing to the tool. But for Central Methodist and the Smiley Library, Pinterest has provided an excellent resource for marketing of collections, information fluency activities, and educational technology classes. As long as interest in Pinterest remains high, this tool will remain a valuable way to present information in a visually appealing and easily accessible format. Its ease of use, functionality, and low cost make it an excellent tool for small libraries who wish to visually present information to their campus community.

REFERENCES

Cold Brew Labs. (2012). *Pinterest terms of service.* San Francisco: Author.

Kessler, S. (2012, June 20). *Mashable social media.* Retrieved from http://mashable .com/2012/06/20/pinterest-attribution/

Tsukayama, H. (2012, March 15). Pinterest address copyright concerns. *Washington Post.*

4

Navigating the Virtual Horizon: Finding Our Way Using Social Media in Hospital Libraries

Yongtao Lin and Kathryn M. E. Ranjit
University of Calgary Libraries

Hospital libraries hold a unique position in health care systems. We are a center for health care professionals to gather the information they need to support their practice and a space for professional development and exploration for adult learners. To fulfill this mandate, hospital libraries need to stay at the cutting edge in learning practices and education technologies. In this chapter, we explore the use of social media in health care, the unique placement of the hospital library in health care systems, and how some hospital libraries are exploring social media. Next, we look at the impact of social media on adult learning. We then reflect on a project that we conducted in a hospital library system, describing how we used social media in creating virtual interest groups for professional development to increase knowledge sharing among librarians, clients, and colleagues and to build a community of practice.

SOCIAL MEDIA AND HEALTH CARE

The recent literature has been inundated with publications about health care and social media. There are numerous examples that include how to implement social media, successful projects, best practices in health care environments, how to interact with the public, and mediating risks. Social media has successfully entered the medical field and has the potential to positively influence health information exchange.

While there are many ways to use social media tools in health care, five clear purposes for social media use by health care professionals and organizations to communicate with the public (Bennett, 2009) have emerged:

- to serve the public better,
- to increase the reach of the message,
- to educate the patient,
- to act as a vehicle for public relations, and
- to communicate in times of crisis.

The specific risks involved when health care organizations or professionals engage in social media can be a deterrent to many. Mitigating the risks may include protecting patient privacy, protecting professional privacy, guarding against miscommunication, and making referrals to traditional communication channels so that messages aren't lost (Bennett, 2009). As long as health care groups navigate with caution and proceed with a plan, risks should not become restraints. Developing a social media policy is recommended as one of the most effective risk mediation techniques. These policies provide guidelines for the use of social media in the organization and define acceptable use of the tools. Examples of well-developed social media policies are available in the Social Media Policy Database, at http://socialmediagovernance.com/policies.php.

SOCIAL MEDIA AND HOSPITAL LIBRARIES

Hospital libraries are slowly adopting social media for many of the same purposes as health care systems when connecting with the public. Libraries engage with clients and offer more effective information service using social platforms, answer questions as a virtual reference service, reach clients through new communication channels, promote services and resources, and communicate notices online (Gebb, 2010). Our placement as a learning center within health care institutions allows for natural synergies in professional development and learning.

Currently, the most popular tools used by hospital libraries include Twitter, blogs, chat, Delicious, and social networking sites. Twitter has been used for reference, as a current awareness vehicle, and for service promotion. Blogs are a common platform for information alert services, for reference services, and as a way for virtual groups to connect (Rethlefsen & Engard, 2007; Tennant et al., 2012). As a result of the information technology restrictions governing many hospital sites, Facebook has not been widely adopted as a social networking platform. However, some libraries are implementing private sites, such as Yammer, or internally developed programs.

SOCIAL MEDIA AND ADULT SOCIAL LEARNING

Online technology has had an enormous impact on society and adult learning. It has been instrumental in setting off the information society, by increasing information mediums, reach, and encouraging information collaboration across disciplines. Adult learning arises from sense making in the information and technology overload, both experientially and socially (Merriam, Caffarella, & Baumgartner, 2007).

Health professionals use the hospital library for professional development or work-based learning. As Williams (2010) emphasizes, learning in this environment needs to be responsive to the skills and knowledge required by the workforce. Courses with a work-based learning philosophy were more useful to the learners and had the potential to change practice and patient care. This learning is context based and requires learners to pay attention to interaction and intersection among people; therefore, knowledge creation and utilization become a collective activity, often referred to as *collective learning*. Collectively, the individuals can discuss, explore, and develop educational content and answer one another's questions. This enhances the engagement of learners with content, as well as their capability to actively learn and collaborate (Bolhuis, 1996).

In many health care settings, staff are expected to explore, experience, and teach themselves new technologies without formal training. The primary characteristics of social media—including accessibility of most social media sites, flexibility in changes, currency of content, and usability of these technologies—help in supporting collective learning–based environments. Even the social media categories (i.e., wikis, blogs, microblogging, media sharing, social bookmarking, social friendship networks, and social news sites; Agarwal, 2011, p. 40) align well with the collective learning model's goals of interactivity and proactivity. While new technology, including social media, reshapes how and what adults learn, adult learning affects the use of technology developments in teaching and learning. More and more learning groups are formed in workplaces using new technologies. Communities of practice and virtual research environments via social media platforms are created to facilitate and support the work-based learning. In the context of a virtual research environment, social networking sites such as Facebook provide an easy means of finding research partners and keeping them in touch with changing interests.

One form of virtual community, the virtual interest group (VIG), is a type of online community that uses social networking sites to allow collaboration among users who are logically grouped with common shared interests (Kallurkar, 2008; Myhill, Shoebridge, & Snook, 2009). Research has shown that the VIGs that were developed and facilitated via social media platforms provide an integrated environment that supports the work of a community or group of collaborating researchers (Voss & Procter, 2009).

OUR STUDY ON USING SOCIAL MEDIA IN CREATING VIGS

Background and Project Objective

Social media may play an integral part in health education and health promotion—however, will it potentially change how health care professionals enhance their learning, seek information, and share knowledge? We decided to conduct a pilot project in two tertiary hospitals in Calgary to examine how Web 2.0 tools enhance interaction between health researchers and librarians and among researchers themselves in an online interest group environment. In addition, we explored whether these tools create a synergistic adult learning experience and increase efficiency in obtaining information or improve quality and quantity of research evidence.

Calgary is the fourth-largest municipality in Canada and the largest in Alberta (Statistics Canada, 2012). The Health Information Network Calgary, a network of hospital libraries located at six major Calgary sites, provides information and library services to patients, the public, and health care professionals working in the Calgary Zone and in cancer care. Promoting collaboration across geographical distances and disciplinary boundaries is one of our primary goals of service.

Clinical practice guidelines and patient safety are two key areas of interest for health researchers. Tailored information services are already in place contributing to the knowledge creation of the groups, including subject-based e-resource guides and current awareness services. These VIGs were made to utilize and improve these existing services. By utilizing social media platforms, our study also chose to look at how content is codeveloped, assessed, and further improved by users.

Research Method

An e-mail invitation was distributed in early June 2011 to the library users in the two sites that were interested in one of the two topics or had requested in-depth literature search support in these areas. A preliminary online survey

(Appendix A) was administered to understand the participants' experience using social media tools, how they used the technologies, and the possible barriers to using these tools for online research purposes. The survey was also intended to help the librarian facilitators identify training needs for the social media tools selected for this study.

Three social media tools were explored in this project:

- A user blog was created using Blogger (http://www.blogspot.com) for each VIG where information about resources that pertained to the topic was posted by both librarians and group members. It also served as a gateway platform for the other two tools integrated into our research group activities.
- Chat rooms were embedded in our blogs, where we connected our group members virtually in real time for subject-related knowledge sharing, information literacy training, and consultation via a browser-based chat service. Two platforms were explored: Meebo (https://www.meebo.com) and Chatroll (http://chatroll.com).
- Delicious bookmarking guides on the interest topics were created and shared via http://www.delicious.com, another tool we linked from the two blogs. Subject tags from those guides allowed researchers to form a number of networks by subscribing to and following the other members.

We also offered three in-person onsite training sessions with interest group members to address any technical issues/concerns about general use of social media and the three tools introduced. A postsurvey (Appendix B) was distributed 3 months later via e-mail to understand their experience using social media in VIGs, gather feedback about the pilot project, assess comfort level with social media tools for research purposes, determine barriers to uptake during the pilot, and seek recommendations for the future services in VIGs.

RESULTS

Presurvey

Twenty-five health care professionals filled out our presurvey, and they indicated interest in participating in our VIG pilot project and learning more about using social media for collaborative learning in one or both of our preselected topics. Most participants had experience with at least one social media tool prior to participation in the VIGs, primarily for communication and information-sharing purposes. Only two participants self-reported discomfort from lack of experience with social media. Self-reported barriers to using social media tools included limited workplace access, time constraints, discomfort with the medium, and privacy issues. Training was requested for creating good online content and for directions to use the tools proposed for the VIGs.

Blog

Twenty-one participants registered for an account with one or both blogs. Twenty posts were published during the 3-month period. Types of information shared in the blog posts included an introduction to each piloted social media tool and "how to" directions, two reviews of articles pertinent to the subject areas, information sharing about tools used in the field, and favorite free resources, including websites and resources created by our participants (e.g., one participant's departmental newsletter).

Chat

Four live chat sessions were held, scheduled approximately every 3 weeks. Eight people participated in one or more the chat sessions. Sessions were an open forum, but each session was prefaced with questions to the group to foster discussions.

> *Session 1:* Troubleshooting issues with signing up for the blogs, why participants were interested in joining the VIGs, social media in health care, and previous experience with the VIG topic.
> *Session 2:* Social media in health care, social media use in parent organization, troubleshooting issues with Delicious.
> *Session 3:* Reflecting on recent posts, using guideline appraisal tools, exploring the use of other social media tools for research and learning purposes.
> *Session 4:* Favorite resources in the VIG topic—websites, medical journals/databases, consultation with colleagues, and so on, and why these are good resources.

Types of information shared in chat sessions included recent developments related to the interest group topic, reflections and discussions about recent posts, interest group resource sharing, discussions about the use of social media for specific information sharing purposes, and new social media tools to explore.

Delicious

The librarian facilitators created three initial bookmark lists (tags) to share with the VIGs: Clinical Practice Guidelines, Patient Safety, and Social Media in Health Care. Twelve participants signed up for Delicious accounts. Participants bookmarked favorite websites during in-person training sessions. Users were encouraged to follow one another's networks. Types of information collected in tag lists included government websites, alert websites, online reports, statistical reports, online appraisal tools, popular reviews, and videos pertaining to the interest group topics.

Postsurvey

Eight participants responded to the postsurvey. These health care professionals reported that having exposure to a tool during the pilot led to more confidence in using these social media tools. Five out of eight respondents were unable to interact with one or more of the social media tools during the pilot. The greatest reported barrier to participation was time constraints.

The blog content was viewed as useful to most participants who read them. Chat sessions were reported as the most useful tool for sharing and discussing interest group resources, as well as for connecting with VIG collaborators and troubleshooting issues. Delicious bookmarking was the most difficult tool to use of those introduced in this pilot. Participants reported that they had difficulty creating accounts for this tool and using it to find useful resources, even after in-person and online training.

Participants joined the VIGs for a variety of reasons (Table 4.1). Most indicated the motivation to learn more about the VIG topics and to connect with their colleagues over these topics. Overall, participants characterized the experience as positive and reported an increased awareness of social media tools for information sharing. Negative experiences noted were due to lack of time available to participate fully.

Table 4.1. Participants' Motivations for Joining the Virtual Interest Group Pilot Study

Motivation	Percentage of Participants (n = 8)
I didn't have any experience in social media so I wanted to learn some basics.	37.5
I had some previous experience with social media and wanted to learn how social media is used for work-related purposes.	25.0
I wanted to be involved in the discussions of the topic(s): patient safety and/or clinical practice guidelines.	62.5
I wanted to be part of the groups to make more connections to people with interest in patient safety and clinical practice guidelines.	50.0
I signed up because the librarian recommended the interest groups and potential benefits to me.	25.0

DISCUSSION

Optimized Information Creation and Knowledge Sharing

While this pilot was social media based, increased information sharing and creation were observed in the VIGs through each social media tool. Some resources that were deemed valuable by this interest group were shared in each tool used in this pilot, such as government websites, online reports, and freely available research tools on the Internet. Information gathering took place when exploring all the different tools but may have been most evident in the chat sessions where questions were addressed in real time. A more stable form of information sharing could be followed later by a blog post or by tagging into Delicious.

Enhanced Relationship Building

The VIG project was designed to introduce the use of social media for creating a collaborative virtual research community, and it was an effort to improve the practice through technology. Participants from different departments and roles at three separate sites came together to participate in the VIGs. The collaborative online environment allowed these professionals to share and learn from others in their organization whom they did not usually have the chance to collaborate with in person. The interactive platforms offered new opportunities for librarians to foster deeper reflection and collaboration from participants and for participants to easily develop networks, relationships, and their identity through information sharing and gathering. As information professionals, we see the potential of social media as a platform for relationship building through collaborative working in which end users and librarians develop services together.

Social Media Training

Social media is gaining an ever-increasing role in health care (Squazzo, 2010). While this pilot was designed to introduce the use of social media for learning and knowledge sharing in health care topics, it was not originally intended to address the prevalence and best practice of social media use in the health care environment. This topic, however, became a recurring theme throughout the pilot. Therefore, through this social learning model, the group adapted the VIGs to address questions in this topic as needed.

Increased Level of Social Media Sophistication for Service Delivery

The firsthand experience and lessons learned from the pilot study have prepared us to use other social media applications that are relevant to libraries to support our integrated information services. For example,

- information discovery and access can be facilitated through the use of bookmarking and blogging;
- reference services extend beyond the physical information desk, where chat is offered as an additional channel;
- teaching and instruction activities can benefit greatly through the inclusion of other types of media and online training sessions; and
- current awareness services have an instant reach through Twitter and blogs.

The following highlights some other social media projects we conducted after the VIG pilot project.

Virtual Reference Service in a Hospital Library Network

Although there is an increase in articles written about the implementation of virtual reference services by chat, most of these are related to university communities, and there is little exploration of what these services look like in the hospital library environment. Exercising what we have learned from online communication through the VIG pilot and incorporating research from online reference studies, we developed a chat reference service for our hospital library network. A recent presentation at the Canadian Health Libraries Association 2012 Conference outlines our implementation strategy for this service, including staff training, usage, and service evaluation (Ranjit, Vaska, & Lin, 2012).

We have also started to explore the use of Twitter for communication updates and reference (http://twitter.com/hinyyc), as well as YouTube for disseminating library tutorials and recommended health information videos (http://www.youtube.com/user/hinyyc), with promising results.

Extending Library Instruction to Collaborate and Connect

An increased understanding of social adult learning theories has provided us with a successful framework for extending library instruction beyond the traditional instruction model to the end users. This framework is meant to focus on learners' self-directed, active learning through exploring and experimenting meaningful education content in social context.

A laddered education curriculum, which consisted of a series of brief courses on various information resources and topics, was developed on the basis of learners' education needs. Although most sessions took place during lunch hours in face-to-face settings, connections were also made through the introduction to follow-up resources available from virtual subject guides to increase the learners' exposure to library resources, to self-paced interactive online modules to enhance learning outcomes, and to more in-person learning sessions to sustain professional development. The program was presented at a national Workshop for Instruction in Library Use in 2012, where the concept of instructing through collaboration and creating social context learning was very well received (Lin & Ranjit, 2012).

Alert Service Using a Blog to Satisfy Researchers' Current Awareness Needs

In April 2012, librarians implemented a current awareness project in cancer care facilities by creating and maintaining a subject-based project to disseminate the latest cancer information in grey literature to the specific research community. The Grey Horizon Blog (http://grey-horizon.blogspot.com) was created in April 2012 using Blogger. The selection and reaggregation of information involves ongoing assessment of user needs and continuous work on the blog. A weekly global e-mail digest listing of the postings was introduced to all staff in July. Since our launch on April 30, 2012, until the end of July 2012, nearly 2,000 page views have been logged for the almost 200 posts that compose our blog thus far. We are planning to evaluate the effectiveness of using a blog for the alert service in October and presented findings at the 14th International Conference in Grey Literature in November 2012 (Lin & Vaska, 2012).

RECOMMENDATIONS

In-Person Training for Online Learning

The intent of the VIG pilot was to facilitate learning in the online environment as much as possible, including training in applying these social media tools. Online learning is increasingly becoming the best practice model for continuing education in health care environment for researchers. However, some participants were unable to take part as desired, perhaps due to the limited time invested in online learning as each tool was introduced. It was observed that facilitated in-person training increased the comfort level and motivation to participate in the VIGs. The introduction of an in-person training session at the outset for learners who prefer this learning style should be considered for conducting similar projects. This also aligns with adult social learning principles in creating interactive, flexible, and multiple learning opportunities.

Training How to Use Social Media Applications

An appreciation is definitely not lacking for end users that there is great potential to the integration of social media in collaborative work and professional development. However, the level of sophistication in the use of these new applications is evidently low, especially for the users whose work is not heavily dependent on information tools, such as health care practitioners. The challenge needs to be addressed by providing continuous couching, training, and troubleshooting on the use of social media tools.

Engaging Organizations and Larger Communities in the Adoption of Social Media

Social media is now contributing to the infrastructure of our everyday activities, not just at home but also at work. Our project has convinced us of the importance of workplace buy-in and stakeholder involvement. This impact was also shown in the results of an Edinburgh Naperi-TFPL study (Hall, Golzari, Blaswick, & Goody, 2008). The study findings revealed that the greatest risks associated with social media applications related to their integration within organizations. They were regarded as "more important than risks to the smooth running and maintenance of information management processes, security, productivity and online citizenship" (Hall, 2011, p. 425).

Another major challenge in workplace settings is the introduction of a tool that has a "social" component as it adds to the perceptions of risks in data security and waste of staff time, especially for librarians working in health services or other public sectors. When access to a social media platform is blocked in a work environment, advocating the value of social media may not be an immediate option. Therefore, rather than taking a tool and considering how it can be implemented, plan the service and identify its value and what is needed to make it work before identifying social media tools that may work within the existing organization infrastructure.

Finally, the service should always involve end users in the development process, whether it is an actual design of a new service or is simply offering additional channels for service delivery. A successful strategy in social media innovation will see end users transformed from consumers to collaborators in building user-generated services with librarians, instead of being part of the traditional information provider-consumer model.

CONCLUSION

Health care providers are quickly adopting social media into their practice. Hospital libraries are in a position where they are both applying these tools for service as well as orienting their clients to use these tools for practice and professional development. The best way to learn is by doing. Find your own way to explore the virtual horizon and provide a good context for collaborative learning and service improvement in your environment.

APPENDIX A: SAMPLE PRESURVEY QUESTIONS
FOR THE VIRTUAL INTEREST GROUP PROJECT

1. Have you had any experience with any Social Media tools, either personally or for work-related purposes?
2. What Social Media tools do you use?
   Flickr
   Twitter
   Delicious
   Facebook
   MySpace
   YouTube
   Ning
   Blogger
   Other
3. How comfortable do you feel while using these Social Media tools?
   Not comfortable at all
   Comfortable
   Very comfortable
4. What do you use these tools for?
   Communication
   Information sharing
   Accessing information
   Creating interest groups or networking
   Marketing or promotion
   Customer service
   Community involvement
   Other
5. How long have you been using these Social Media tools (any tool)?
   Less than a year
   Between a year and three years
   Longer than three years
6. If you haven't been using Social Media tools, please share with us why, either at work or in your personal life.
7. Do you have any concerns about using Social Media tools for work-related purposes?
   No concerns
   Lack of time
   Not supported by the organization
   Can't access these tools from the work computer
   Not sure how to create good content
   Concern about information privacy

Legal risks
Other
8. What type(s) of learning opportunities can we provide to help you feel comfortable participating in this project?
   Online class
   Online tutorials
   In-person training
   Handouts
   No training needed
   Other
9. In what topic(s) would training be useful?
   Blogging
   Creating good content
   Using bookmarks
   Other
10. Do you have any other questions or comments about Social Media?

APPENDIX B: SAMPLE POSTSURVEY QUESTIONS FOR THE VIRTUAL INTEREST GROUP PROJECT

1. Can you share with us why you were interested in participating in our interest groups?
   I didn't have any experience with Social Media and wanted to learn the basics
   I had some previous experience and want to learn how Social Media is used for work-related purposes
   I wanted to be involved in the discussions of the topic(s): patient safety and/or clinical practice guidelines
   I wanted to be part of the groups to make more connections to people with interest in patient safety and clinical practice guidelines
   I signed up because the librarian recommended the interest groups and potential benefits to me
   Other

Blogs

2. Did you create an account for any of the two blogs?
3. Have you read any of the blog posts in VIG blogs?
4. Did you find information from the blogs useful?
5. If you did not create an account for the blogs, can you share with us why?
6. Other comments

Delicious

7. Did you create an account for Delicious?
8. Did you find any useful website from Delicious?
9. If you did not create an account in Delicious, can you share with us why?
10. Other comments

Chat

11. Did you attend any of the chat room sessions?
12. What characteristics of the chat session(s) did you find useful?
    Connecting with other members of the VIG
    Sharing and discussing a useful interest group resource
    Troubleshooting an issue with interest group Social Media tools
    I didn't find the chat session useful
    Other
13. If you did not attend a chat session, can you share with us why?
14. How comfortable do you feel now while using these Social Media tools, compared to before participating in our project?
    More comfortable
    Still not comfortable
    No change
15. What would you use these tools for in the future?
    Communication
    Information sharing
    Accessing information
    Creating interest groups or networking
    Marketing or promotion
    Customer service
    Community involvement
    Other
16. Other comments

REFERENCES

Agarwal, N. (2011). Collective learning: An integrated use of social media in learning environment. In B. White, I. King, & P. Tsang (Eds.), *Social media tools and platforms in learning environments* (pp. 37–51). New York: Springer.

Bennett, E. (2009). *Hospitals and social media: A survey of best practices.* Retrieved from http://www.slideshare.net/edbennett/hospitals-social-media

Bolhuis, S. (1996). *Towards active and selfdirected learning: Preparing for lifelong learning, with reference to Dutch secondary education.* Retrieved from http://

ezproxy.lib.ucalgary.ca:2048/login?url=http://search.ebscohost.com/login.aspx ?direct=true&db=eric&AN=ED396141&site=ehost-live

Gebb, B. A. (2010). *Social media for medical librarians.* Retrieved from http://www .slideshare.net/FrontierLibrary/social-media-for-medical-librarians.

Hall, H. (2011). Relationship and role transformations in social media environments. *Electronic Library, 29*, 421–428.

Hall, H., Golzari, S., Blaswick, B., & Goody, M. (2008). *Opportunity and risk in social computing environments.* Retrieved from http://www.soc.napier.ac.uk/~hazelh/ esis/soc_comp_proj_rep_public.pdf

Kallurkar, S. (2008). Targeted information dissemination. *DTIC Online.* Retrieved from http://www.dtic.mil/cgi-bin/GetTRDoc?AD=ADA480150&Location=U2 &doc=GetTRDoc.pdf

Lin, Y., & Ranjit, K. M. E. (2012). Designing a sustainable information literacy curriculum for health care professionals in a hospital library network. In *Forty-first Annual Workshop for Instruction in Library Use.* Retrieved from http://sites .macewan.ca/wilu2012/files/2012/06/May23_1600_LinRanjit_DesigningSustain ableInformation.pdf

Lin, Y., & Vaska, M. (2012). Creating and assessing a subject-based blog for current awareness within a cancer care environment. In *Fourteenth International Conference on Grey Literature.* Retrieved from http://www.textrelease.com/gl14program/ session3.html

Merriam, S. B., Caffarella, L. M., & Baumgartner, R. S. (2007). *Learning in Adulthood: A Comprehensive Guide* (3rd ed.). San Francisco: Jossey-Bass.

Myhill, M., Shoebridge, M., & Snook, L. (2009). Virtual research environments— A Web 2.0 cookbook?" *Library Hi Tech, 27*(2), 228–238.

Ranjit, K. M. E., Vaska, M., & Lin, Y. (2012, June). *Evaluating a chat reference service in a hospital library network.* Paper presented at the Thirty-Sixth Annual Canadian Health Libraries Association/Association Des Bibliothèques De La Santé Du Canada Conference, Hamilton, ON. Retrieved from http://www.chla -absc.ca/2012/images/slides/chla2012_paper_presentation_ranjit.pdf

Rethlefsen, M. L., & Engard, N. C. (2007). Social software for libraries and librarians. *Journal of Hospital Librarianship.* Retrieved from http://www.tandfonline .com/doi/abs/10.1300/J186v06n04_03

Squazzo, J. D. (2010). Best practices for applying social media in healthcare. *Healthcare Executive, 25*(3), 34–36, 38–39.

Statistics Canada. (2012). *Table 5: Most populous municipalities (census subdivisions) by province and territory, 2011.* Retrieved from http://www12.statcan.gc.ca/ census-recensement/2011/as-sa/98-310-x/2011001/tbl/tbl5-eng.cfm

Tennant, M. R., Auten, B., Botero, C. E., Butson, L. C., Edwards, M. E., Garcia-Milian, R., et al. (2012). Changing the face of reference: Adapting biomedical and health information services for the classroom, clinic, and beyond. *Medical Reference Services Quarterly, 31*, 280–301.

Voss, A., & Procter, R. (2009). Virtual research environments in scholarly work and communications. *Library Hi Tech, 27*(2), 174–190.

Williams, C. (2010). Understanding the essential elements of work-based learning and its relevance to everyday clinical practice. *Journal of Nursing Management, 18*, 624–632.

5

Beyond the Teen Space:
Reaching Teens through Social Media

Laura A. Horn
The Farmington Public Libraries

THE FARMINGTON LIBRARIES TEEN SPACE:
A BRIEF INTRODUCTION

The Farmington Library is located directly in front of the Farmington High School, which serves all of Farmington, Connecticut. On any given afternoon during the academic year, approximately 30 teens use the Teen Space to browse the shelves, use the iMacs, play Wii games, or just hang out with their friends. These teens are usually in the space from 2:30 PM until 4:00 PM or 5:30 PM, depending on which late bus they take or when their friends leave. There are eight iMacs in the Teen Space, a Wii console with a large flatscreen mounted on the wall, comfy chairs for hanging out, and café-style tables and chairs for teens who wish to do homework or play games with their friends. There is also a computer lab with 10 Dell computers adjacent to the Teen Space, which I open for teens when it isn't already being used for a library program. The majority of teens who come to the Teen Space in the afternoons are high school students. I have been told that there used to be a bus that dropped the middle school students off at the library in the afternoons, but that hasn't happened since I have worked at the library.

GETTING STARTED

In July 2010, just 2 months after graduating from Simmons with my master's degree, I was offered a paid internship at 25 hours per week at the main branch of the Farmington Libraries. I was going to be filling in for the teen librarian while she was out on leave. Over the course of the next 6 months or so, I was to staff the Teen Space in the afternoons from about 2:30 until 5:00 (when I left for the day), maintain the teen collections, plan programs, and update the teen department's various social media outlets as necessary. In addition to my responsibilities to the teen department, I staffed the reference desk between 8 and 15 hours per week, which fluctuated depending on whether I was working on a Saturday. Between the time that I spent staffing the Teen Space and my time spent staffing the reference desk, I had approximately 4.5 hours per week to devote to collection development and maintenance, planning programs, and updating the various social media platforms that the teen librarian usually used. With so little time, I knew that I needed to prioritize, but I wasn't sure where to begin. Where should I focus my attention? What does this library value, and how can I contribute to those values? I turned to the libraries' mission statement:

> The Farmington Library is a comfortable, dynamic environment where current technology, friendly, professional service, equal access to a wide variety of materials, and cultural, educational and recreational programs encourage the exchange of ideas, kindle the pleasure of reading and life-long learning, preserve the memories and history of Farmington and its neighbors, and foster community spirit. We are Farmington's Living Room.

Okay, so we are Farmington's living room, but if we aren't close to people's homes and they can't drive (like most teens), then how do they know what the library has to offer? My job was to make sure that teens and their parents knew what programs were happening and when, as well as what materials the library had to offer teens. Since only a small portion of the teen population was actually coming to the Teen Space to hang out on a regular basis, I knew that I needed to go to them, and I knew that the best way to do this was to reach out to them online.

According to the Pew Research Center's Internet & American Life Project's 2011 Teen/Parent Survey (2012), 80% of American teens use an online social networking site, such as MySpace or Facebook, and an additional 16% use Twitter. This means that there is a wonderful opportunity to build relationships with teens in the community and market library services to them for free.

MARKETING IS NOT A DIRTY WORD

For many, *marketing* is a dirty word. They think of sales people and those annoying Internet advertisements that pop up trying to sell you things you don't want or need. Marketing, however, is quite necessary for any entity that offers goods or services of any kind. Being a nonprofit does not make you exempt from marketing. Sure, there will always be the regulars that come to the library for the latest Patterson book or to use the computers, but what about the rest of the population that doesn't come to the library regularly? In most towns, there are far more people who don't come to the library regularly than there are people who do. If the Farmington Library and, specifically, the Teen Space were to become a center of learning and community, then I needed to show the community what the library had to offer its teens. This included marketing the space, the collection, and the programs.

Anyone who has ever marketed a product or service before knows that you need to meet your target audience where they are, on their terms. Thanks to my predecessors, a teen librarian Facebook account was already in place when I began, and we had a healthy number of friends, over 200 if I remember correctly. There was also a teen department blog hosted by Blogger and a teen review blog hosted by WordPress. The Facebook account was used primarily to interact with teens through status updates about the library and by sharing photos of teens hanging out at the library or attending library programs. The teen department blog was used mostly to inform the Farmington community as a whole about teen programs taking place at the library, and the WordPress blog was used exclusively to post teen-authored book reviews. We have also allowed teens to post reviews of movies and music, but it is mainly used for sharing book reviews.

I had great tools to use but little time to actually devote to them, and I knew from the hours that I spent in graduate classes that the keys to making any social media outlet successful were consistency, frequency, and relevancy. With my schedule being as busy as it was, I decided to choose one social media outlet at a time. After I felt comfortable with one, I would move on to the next. When I finally had a handle on managing all three of the three tools already in place, I would look to new outlets for marketing.

To get started, one does need to have at the very least a basic knowledge of the tools one is going to use, and one needs to be comfortable with working in a tech environment that is constantly changing. Fortunately for me, I had used blogs and microblogs while in graduate school, and I had my own Facebook account, so I didn't need any formal training before I got started. I had enough basic knowledge to get by, and everything else I learned by experience. If you or a member of your staff is going to begin outreach efforts to the community via social media tools, make sure to have some basic knowledge of how things work, or seek advice from those around you. There are many wonderful librarians on listservs that would be more than happy to help a fellow librarian, not to mention the wealth of information that can be found online and in print about using social media sites as marketing tools.

BEGINNING WITH FACEBOOK

I decided to start with Facebook for one simple reason: more than half of American teens are using social networking sites such as Facebook and MySpace (Pew Research Center's Internet & American Life Project, 2012). I know the Pew report included MySpace, but I haven't met one teen in Farmington who uses MySpace, at least not exclusively.

I began my Facebook campaign by trying to post my status updates in the mornings while I had time at my desk, before the teens got to the library. However, I quickly realized that there were very few teens online at that time since they were in school. You'd think this would have been obvious right from the start, but it had been nearly a decade since I was in high school, and I had happily forgotten that being in high school meant sitting in classrooms from about 7:30 in the morning until about 2:30 in the afternoon. With Facebook and most other social media outlets, timing is everything. If you are posting when no one is around to read your posts, then you might as well quit. It's akin to giving a speech to an empty room. I had to make time to reach out to the teens when they were available.

I noticed that most of the teens who came to the library after school left by about 4:00 PM and I worked until 5:00 PM. I figured that I had 1 hour of prime Facebook time with these teens. During that time, I would make myself available to chat; I would create events, send out invites, and post status updates about items newly added to the collection. Almost immediately after shifting the time of day that I posted my status updates, I started getting comments and responses to my event invites. I also tracked the click-throughs on the links that I posted on Facebook. I did this by using bitly.com to generate shortened links, which then enabled me to look at those links and see how many times they had been clicked on. If I noticed that teens weren't clicking the links to online writing contests, I would stop posting links to online writing contests. My momentum was building, and ensuring that my content was relevant to the teens was integral in maintaining this momentum.

In addition to increased interaction with my current friends, I started receiving more friend requests from Farmington teens. Not only was Facebook enabling me to connect with teens online whom I had never interacted with before, but it was also facilitating introductions in person. On numerous occasions I have been approached by teens in the Teen Space who say, "You're that library lady on Facebook aren't you?" "Yes I am, and you are?" Instant introduction—thank you very much, Facebook.

At this point, I was happy with how things were progressing with the Facebook account, and I was ready to move on to the blogs.

IMPLEMENTING YOUR OWN FACEBOOK PROGRAM

Facebook is an ever-changing environment, so in addition to keeping your account up-to-date with posts and events, you need to read articles online about Facebook and what changes may be coming or what changes have recently taken place. Other things that you should know about Facebook follow (these are some general guidelines, not hard-and-fast rules):

1. You will need to decide if you will create a page, group, or personal account or some combination of the three. Do a little research before you choose which type of account you will use. See what other libraries or businesses have done, and determine which aspects will or will not work for your purposes.
2. Don't use an avatar or gimmicky photo of yourself as your profile picture. Teens like to know whom they are interacting with, especially if you are an adult.
3. Don't post on teens' walls—not even if you see them every day and think they like you a lot.
4. Do use Facebook as a way to communicate with teens through status updates, event invites, or private messages. I have found that many teens prefer messaging on Facebook to sending e-mail. If you have any library clubs or groups, create a Facebook group. This is how I connect with my Teen Advisory Group members between meetings. I am able to remind them of meetings and ask them for input on the next meeting's agenda.
5. Choose your friends wisely, and create lists. If you create a page, this isn't really a concern, but if you choose to use a personal account or a group, this is important. I try to keep my teen space, both physical and virtual, adult-free, with the few exceptions being coworkers, fellow librarians, and teens who have graduated. I then create lists in Facebook, which enable me to target specific subsets of my friends when posting updates.

MOVING BEYOND FACEBOOK: THE BLOGOSPHERE

Blogger and WordPress

Facebook is wonderful, but there are tasks that are better accomplished using other tools, such as blogs. Since I have chosen to use a personal Facebook account, which enables me to select my friends strategically, I am purposely leaving out large segments of the population that I don't necessarily want to ignore altogether. For instance, it is important for the Friends of the Library, the Library Board, local media outlets, and the nonteen portion of the town of Farmington to know what the library has to offer local teens.

The teen page of the libraries' website is a great tool for telling people what the library has to offer. Here I can post dates and times of upcoming events and offer an overview of what the physical Teen Space has to offer. What I cannot is post updates to the website as fast as I can update a blog or microblog.

Blogs offer the unique opportunity to easily post photos, videos, and text. The teen department has two separate blogs with very separate purposes. The first is the teen department's blog, which is hosted by Blogger (http://farm ingtonlibctteen.blogspot.com). The purpose of the teen department's blog is to show the community what the Teen Space has to offer. Sometimes this means that we post pictures of teens at programs; sometimes, the pictures are of teens volunteering; and other times, the pictures are of teens just hanging out in the Teen Space. This blog also acts as a living visual history of the teen department. People who visit the blog are able to see pictures from a program that happened yesterday, as well as pictures of a program that happened 1 year ago.

In the past, the teen department blog was also used to post book trailers and highlight books in the teen collection. However, since I could and often did post book trailers on Facebook, I felt like I was duplicating my efforts. What value was I adding if all of my social media outlets were sharing the same information? This was when I decided to only use the Blogger blog for posting photos. I then enabled the "Share It" widget, which allowed blog readers to share posts on Facebook and Twitter. Now when I post photos from programs on the blog, I can share them on Facebook for teens to see and on the @FarmLibTeen Twitter account.

The teen review blog (http://farmingtonlibraryteenreviews.wordpress .com), which is hosted by WordPress, is an important tool for marketing the collection, as well as empowering teens. During the academic year, a teen volunteer comes in once a week after school and writes reviews of books she has recently read. During the summer, the reviews published are submitted by Farmington teens as part of our Summer Reading Challenge. This summer, teens earned one raffle ticket for our grand prize drawing for each review they wrote or book trailer they created using any medium they chose. The reviews were then posted to the blog by teen volunteers who added book cover images for the item being reviewed and a link to the item in the libraries' catalog. I linked this blog to the @FarmLibTeen Twitter account so that each time a new review was published, a Tweet would be sent out and then posted to Facebook. This enabled me to reach people who read blogs as well the people who follow us on Twitter and all of our teen friends on Facebook.

Things to keep in mind when blogging:

1. Know your audience. Who are you trying to reach? If you are trying to reach teens, how are you going to get them to your blog? You may want to add a widget such as "Share It" or post a link to your blog on your website. Maybe you want to post flyers in your library with a link or a QR code that will take people to your blog. I see teens on Facebook far more often than I see them reading blogs, so if you are using this as your only marketing tool, you will really need to get the word out in your community.
2. Update, update, update. We all fall into a rut every now and then where we don't post nearly as often as we should. With blogs, it is especially important to update them frequently. The worst thing is visiting a blog only to find that the last post was published a year ago. The owner might publish a new exciting article tomorrow, but you will probably never go back to see it. And why would you? There are so many blogs that stay current; there is no need to spend time with those that do not.
3. Make sure that you make your blog visible to everyone and indexable by search engines. If you turn these features off, people won't be able to find your blog.

Microblogging with Twitter

I set up a Twitter account early in 2011. My reason for doing this was that I knew it was an easy way to get small bits of information to large groups of people quickly. I also knew that I could follow young adult authors and publishers and retweet news that I thought would interest local teens, such as book giveaways, writing contests, and author appearances. I decided to start by connecting my new Twitter account with my Facebook account so that teens would see that I was on Twitter. This way, I could post on Twitter, and my tweets would appear on my Facebook wall and in the timelines of my followers, thereby alerting teens to the fact that I was on Twitter. The reaction I hoped for was "That's awesome! The teen librarian is on Twitter. I'm going to follow her." This was not, however, the reaction I received. After months of tweeting, I had over 30 followers, but none of them were teens. Most of my followers were authors, other libraries and librarians or local media. This led me to believe that perhaps teens weren't using Twitter yet. I knew that when I started using Twitter a couple years ago, most teens had no idea what it was; maybe this was still the case. I would soon realize that this was not the case. Teens, specifically Farmington teens, were absolutely using Twitter—they just weren't following me.

One afternoon, I asked one of my regular teens about Twitter. Would he ever follow the teen librarian? His answer, "no." Not "maybe" or "let me think about it" but flat-out "no." According to him, teens feel that they can be truly anonymous on Twitter. They used to feel this way on Facebook, but then their parents, aunts, uncles, librarians, and everyone else jumped on the bandwagon and ruined their little piece of heaven. Now they are migrating to Twitter in droves. I asked him if he would consider following me if I promised not to follow him back. This seemed like a simple and reasonable solution. That way, he would be able to see my posts, but I wouldn't see his. Again, the answer was "no." His reason: the number of people you follow needs to be almost the same as the number of people who follow you. If you follow more people than follow you, you aren't cool. What could I say to that? I don't want anyone losing his popularity status for me.

Twitter may not be the next-best thing for marketing to teens, but it might, and I won't know if I don't stick with it for at least a little while longer. While it hasn't enabled me to reach more teens directly, I have found it to be a great tool for getting news about upcoming teen programs out into the community, so for now, I will continue to post updates on Twitter. Maybe some parents will see a tweet about an event coming up for teens and pass the message on to their children. This may not have been my initial goal, but it does work well. You can't be afraid to try new things and adapt your strategies as necessary. It is, however, important to stick with these initiatives once you begin, even if your initial results aren't what you hoped for. We didn't make over 260 friends on Facebook overnight—why should Twitter be any different?

HOW MUCH IS THIS GOING TO COST?

The online tools themselves are free, which is wonderful, but the technology you need to use those tools is not. Anyone who has access to a computer with an Internet connection can start connecting online with teens (or any other target population). I have, however, included a list of tools similar to those that I use on a daily basis. These items will enable you to successfully start and maintain a social media program. There are, of course, more and less expensive options in all categories—what you purchase will depend on your budget and your specific needs.

- The New iPad, 16gb, wi-fi model ($499)
- InCase iPad case ($60)
- Zagg Invisible SHIELD Smudge-Proof for Apple iPad2—it works with the New iPad as well ($40)

- AppleCare+ for iPad ($99)
- Dell Optiplex 790 (starting at $529; Dell, 2012)
- Canon Powershot A2300 from B&H Photo ($119; B&H Foto & Electronics Corp, 2012)

My favorite gadget that I absolutely would not want to live without is my iPad. Of course, it isn't a necessity, but it does make my job a lot easier. If I am occupied in the Teen Space all afternoon with no time to get to my computer, I simply log-in to my Facebook app and do what I need to do. The built-in camera allows me to take pictures of programs while they are taking place, and if an altercation arises in the Teen Space, I am easily able to photograph the teens involved to alert other staff members. The Pages app allows me to create documents and then e-mail them to myself in Word format to be opened on my PC. If a teen is looking for a particular book, I can connect to the catalog and find the item for him or her without ever having to leave the Teen Space. While the iPad is certainly a luxury item, it is extremely useful.

ASSESSING THE EFFICACY OF YOUR SOCIAL MEDIA TOOLS

Most of the tools you will use have their own programs for tracking statistics. Blogger and WordPress both show you how many visits your blog has had on specific dates. This enables you to see if certain days or weeks are more popular. With Blogger you can also see which posts received the most traffic, and you can see where your readers are being referred from. WordPress also shows you what sites are referring readers to your blog.

Twitter and Facebook are a bit trickier. You never know if someone reads one of your posts unless he or she comments on it or clicks on a link that you have created using a site such as bitly.com. If, however, you have a Facebook page instead of a personal account, you will receive e-mail with your weekly statistics, and you can check your statistics anytime by logging in to your account. This option is not offered to personal accounts, since individuals who are not marketing a product or service are not typically concerned with statistical data. This is another thing to take into consideration when deciding what type of Facebook account to create.

In addition to gathering information from the statistics given to you by the tools, you can gain a great deal of insight by surveying your target population. A great way to do this with teens is to visit the schools in your town. Ask if you can come and introduce yourself to the teens and do a book talk. During your introduction, tell the teens a little about your Facebook or Twitter account, and how they might benefit from friending or following you. Then hand out a short survey. On the survey you could ask teens the following:

1. Before today did you know that the teen librarian had a Facebook account?
   a. Yes
   b. No
2. Are you already friends with the teen librarian? If yes, skip to number 4.
   a. Yes
   b. No
3. Now that you know that the teen librarian has a Facebook account would you friend her?
   a. Yes
   b. No. If no, why?
4. What type of information should the teen librarian post on her Facebook account to make it interesting to teens? Circle any that apply.
   a. Library programs for teens
   b. New books for teens
   c. Community events that may interest teens
   d. New media such as video games, CDs and DVDs
   e. Other:

It is always good to check with your target audience every once in a while, just like it is important to review the statistics from your blogs or Facebook. You may learn that something that was once very popular is now growing out of fashion and something that gained little momentum early on is now becoming the most popular tool. The web and all things on it are fluid. New technologies and websites come and go, and it is up to you to follow the trends. This means knowing when to adopt a new tool or when to pass on something that will be a fleeting fad. It also means not being afraid to try something new when you know that it may not work.

GOING FORWARD

My goals for this coming year are to attract more teen followers on both Twitter and Facebook and to enlist another regular blogger for the teen review blog. To do this, I will employ a few different techniques. I would like to start by visiting classes at the high school and the middle school to conduct book-talks and spread the word about my Facebook and Twitter accounts. At this time, I will also host random giveaways on both Facebook and Twitter to give teens an additional incentive to friend or follow me.

There are some great, highly anticipated books coming out this fall that would make wonderful prizes.

To find another blogger, I will do some old-fashioned asking around. I found my current blogger by approaching a teen who regularly stopped by the Teen Space to grab a pile of books. I asked her if she would like to write reviews and, in turn, she would receive credit for community service, which looks great on college applications. I also offered to write recommendation letters or serve as a professional reference when necessary. This brings me to my final and most important point.

Whatever you are trying to accomplish, it can't be all about you and furthering your cause. It has to be about your audience, and in my case, that audience is Farmington's teens. I'm not just marketing the library to them. I'm interacting with them and learning about what they enjoy and what they want and need. I am offering them opportunities to learn more about themselves and the community they live in. The teens in turn are letting me into their lives, and that is not something that I take lightly. Teens need responsible adults in their lives who respect them, not just in person, but in the virtual world as well.

REFERENCES

B&H Foto & Electronics Corp. (2012). *Canon PowerShot A2300 digital camera (black)*. Retrieved from http://www.bhphotovideo.com/bnh/controller/home?O=&sku=842870&Q=&is=REG&A=details

Dell. (2012). *OptiPlex 790 desktop*. Retrieved from http://www.dell.com/us/slgov/p/optiplex-790/pd

Pew Research Center's Internet & American Life Project. (2012). *2011 Teen/Parent Survey*. Retrieved from http://pewinternet.org/Trend-Data-(Teens)/Online-Activites-Total.aspx

6

The Library in the Social Network: Twitter at the Vancouver Public Library

Kay Cahill
The Vancouver Public Library

As the web becomes a more social and porous medium, remember that interaction and community are going to happen with or without your involvement. You can watch the conversation take place, or you can own and guide it.

—Adam Weinroth

In 2004, Harvard student Mark Zuckerberg and a handful of his friends and roommates created a simple social networking tool called Facebook. Initially restricted to college students, the site opened its doors to the world in 2006. During the same year, Jack Dorsey created and launched the micro-blogging site Twitter. In 2012, the sites had a combined total of 1.4 billion active users: 900 million on Facebook and 500 million on Twitter. Photo-sharing site Flickr has developed a user base of 51 million members and more than 6 billion unique images since its inception in 2007. YouTube, which launched in 2005, now contains more than 1.3 billion videos that were viewed over 1 trillion times in 2011.

Of course, social media was around before Facebook, Twitter, Flickr, and YouTube. Friendster, MySpace, Orkut, Livejournal, and others rose, fell, were swallowed up by competitors, or settled for small but stable niche audiences. But Facebook was the site that really changed the game, pushing social media into the mainstream and blurring the lines between traditional marketing and the online spaces where individuals connected with friends and shared content with one another. The shifts in user behavior happened rapidly, posing interesting questions for libraries as they kept a watchful professional eye on the changing technological landscape. Was there a place for the public library as an organization in these online spaces? Could libraries really add value to their services by creating social media accounts? And how could institutions, not traditionally known for their ability to move quickly, establish themselves in an environment that was evolving at such a tremendous pace?

At the Vancouver Public Library (VPL), we believed that the answer to the first and second questions was a definite yes and that the third was something we could address with the right approach. In early 2008, the first VPL social networking accounts were created on Facebook and Twitter, and we began exploring the potential of these new tools for promoting our services and building connections with our patrons.

ABOUT VPL

VPL is the largest library system in the province of British Columbia and the third-largest system in Canada. It has 22 branches and 275,000 registered cardholders; it contains over 2 million items in its print collections; and in 2011, it answered more than 900,000 reference questions. Patrons came to our branches more than 6.5 million times last year and visited http://www.vpl.ca just under 5 million times. The City of Vancouver and its residents continue to provide strong support for library services.

VPL's website underwent a full-scale redesign and relaunch in 2008, with the goal of becoming a true virtual branch rather than a static collection of pages. A brand new teen site followed in 2009, and in 2011 the library's collection of online subject guides was moved into a new content platform, LibGuides, which allowed for flexible, web-friendly presentation of content. An ongoing goal for the site is to create opportunities not just to present content but to create opportunities for dialogue, interaction, and connection with the community.

FROM PILOT TO PRACTICE

The 2008 website redesign gave a small nod to the increasing prominence of social media sites. An Events Archive provided the option of linking to YouTube footage and Flickr photographs from library programs, and Delicious was used as a repository for the library's extensive collections of annotated links. However, these efforts were still firmly focused on sharing the library's content with virtual visitors, not with engaging those visitors in dialogue about that content. Social networking sites—specifically, Twitter and Facebook—provided a means of bridging this gap, but these were not the communication vehicles that had been intended for the new website. The tools that were recommended for creating discussion space were much more traditional: four branch blogs hosted on our own web servers and embedded into branch pages, with the option for users to comment on posts.

The *ah-ha* moment that led us away from the blogs and into social networking sites was a preliminary investigation into Twitter hashtags. From this, we learned that VPL was already a hot topic on Twitter. Patrons were tweeting about the treasures they had discovered on the shelves at our book sale, having animated discussions about library programs while sitting in the audience at events, and grumbling about the speed of the wi-fi connection at the Central Library. Out there, on the web, we were already the subject of conversation—but at this point, it was not a conversation in which we were participating.

The branch blogs had proved more problematic to implement than we expected, with firewall security issues affecting the ability for users to submit comments. Now we had another option and one that came with significant benefits. The social networking community was already established in its chosen venues and showing an active interest in our services. There would be no need to try to drive traffic to our own site, and we would be able to respond to questions and give the library an opportunity to participate in conversations on which it could currently only eavesdrop. At the same time, this represented a shift from our traditional focus on a single library website where we owned and controlled both the content and the hardware used to host it. Organizationally, we had a way to go before we would be ready to accept that social media was not just a useful addition to the virtual toolbox but a primary means of communication in and of itself.

Twitter and Facebook virtually self-selected themselves as the best platforms for an initial foray into social networking. Our goals were to find tools that we believed had the potential to assist us in engaging both current users and nonusers of the library, to identify spaces where there was already a community connection or interest in the library and its services, and to keep the workload involved in running pilot accounts to a manageable level since at this point no additional resources were available. Two members of staff, the assistant manager for website and community development and the web services librarian, were initially the only administrators for these accounts and were responsible for creating 100% of the content.

In early 2008, libraries were only just beginning to enter the social networking space, and those that did so were, for the most part, out on their own. At the beginning of a phenomenon, there are no best practices to follow, no recommended path, no guidelines for success or failure. This was slightly daunting in that we couldn't be certain that our approach would work, but it was also very exciting because it meant that our options were wide open.

Our two greatest concerns were that we create an accessible, friendly on-line presence that would encourage interaction and dialogue and that we use social media tools to bring real value to our patrons and our services rather than just jumping on the bandwagon because it was the "in thing" for libraries to be doing. To achieve the former, we focused on creating a very distinctive voice for the organization. The librarians behind the posts never self-identi-fied but took care to use the first-person plural; they also made a conscious effort to intersperse funny or quirky facts about the library with the posts, relaying important service information or promoting new library resources. Laughing at our own (occasional) typos also proved to be a winning formula: "Who knew librarians could be so funny!" said one poster after a brief ex-change when a URL shortener botched the link we were trying to share.

Right from the start, the chosen communities reacted with enthusiasm. "I'm very happy to see you on Twitter Vancouver Public Library," com-mented one Twitter user shortly after the account was set up. "I wish you the best moving forward into the new. Respect." "Loving the way you're using Twitter," added another. With the number of Twitter followers and Facebook fans growing daily, the power of the connections we were establishing with social networks soon became apparent. Early successes included a petition in support of provincial library funding, which was retweeted in less than an hour by @VPL followers with a combined total of more than 9,000 followers of their own; a comment about the lack of recycling bins at the Kensington Branch, which was acted on immediately after being forwarded to the branch head; and the use of Twitter (via a cell phone) for emergency communica-tions when an explosion in a BC Hydro substation left downtown Vancouver without power and temporarily knocked out the library's web servers.

As well as being a great platform for broadcasting information about the library, the new social networking tools quickly proved both a powerful means of creating community connections and an excellent venue for establishing dialogue and engaging with patrons. When a patron who had been living abroad returned to Vancouver and tweeted about how much she had missed the library, @VPL tweeted back that the library had missed her too. The delighted patron responded, "If this had been my childhood, it'd be like Santa writing back!" This informal, welcoming human face of the organization brought practical benefits, too: After a concerned patron was assisted with some outstanding fines via Twitter, the person sent a grateful message expressing being too afraid to approach staff in person because of the amount of money involved but felt able to enquire on Twitter because @VPL seemed "so friendly."

Another valuable and unexpected outcome was the realization that, through Twitter, we were reaching current nonlibrary users, particularly among the technology savvy in their twenties and thirties. A common theme raised by these users was that they had previously held the traditional view of the library as very printcentric, without much to offer their demographic. Seeing the library on Twitter caused them to rethink this view and begin exploring some of the new digital services, such as the BiblioCommons catalogue interface and the online subscription databases. "Had no idea the library offered something like this—thanks!!!" posted one user after following a link in a library tweet to the Naxos streaming music database.

The importance of our involvement in the online conversations about the library was emphasized not just by our increased ability to promote both new and existing services but our ability to step in swiftly to correct mistakes and misinformation. In the aftermath of the 2011 Stanley Cup riot, a Twitter user who claimed to be a friend of a relative of a librarian reported that the Children's Library had been completely destroyed during the night of violence. As the false rumor spread, the web team was able to respond quickly, stemming the tide by using the @VPL account to clarify that the Children's Library had experienced a single broken window and was just fine after a cleanup by maintenance staff.

The staff working on the Twitter account reported creating content and responding to patrons' tweets to be both rewarding and fun (Figure 6.1). During this early phase, the work was still done in the odd minutes between other tasks, highlighting another benefit of Twitter: the workload is scalable. An initial presence can be established and maintained even when time is limited. However, as the popularity of the @VPL account increased, it became clear that it was going to need more time, more effort, and a more structured and strategic administrative approach to reach its full potential.

Figure 6.1. Vancouver Public Library Twitter feed with custom background.

MOVING TO CENTER STAGE

At the time of writing, the VPL Twitter account recently passed the 9,000 mark, representing around 3% of VPL's cardholders. A rotating team of four staff members monitors the account daily, posting responses to patron queries, updating the account with new tweets, and using the HootSuite administrative tool (http://www.hootesuite.com) to schedule posts at times or dates when the library isn't open or no web team members are available. Topics include library and community events, library news, information about library resources (e.g., guides, databases, and apps), related news from the wider publishing and technology worlds, and, of course, the odd funny post or picture (like the cucumber that mysteriously showed up in the lost-and-found one afternoon). The web team also updates VPL's main Facebook account several times daily and provides support and guidance for the administrators of the seven branch Facebook pages.

So how did VPL move from two staff running pilot Twitter and Facebook accounts off the side of their desks to this much more structured and committed approach to social media? At the time when the account was created, libraries were very new to social networks. There were no statistics to share to show the effectiveness of tweets or Facebook posts as a means of community engagement, because these services hadn't been established for long enough to evaluate (though this would soon change). In the library world in general, the early adopters were busy climbing on board while the majority wondered whether this was just another passing bandwagon and whether it was appropriate or worthwhile for libraries to be on social networks at all.

As the pilot progressed through 2008, the VPL account quickly accumulated the greatest number of followers of any Canadian public library on Twitter and entered the overall "Twitter Library League" top 10. The number of followers regularly doubled from month to month as the account's popularity grew and enthusiastic fans retweeted library posts or urged their followers to add @VPL as part of the weekly Follow Friday (#FF) recommendations.

As awareness of the account's popularity spread through the library, other departments and branches began to submit requests to have specific services and events promoted via Twitter. The web team and the marketing and communications department also began posting press releases and other important organizational updates on social media as well as through standard communication channels.

The effect of the increase in followers and content was twofold. First, it highlighted the need for proper tools to assist with account management to assign the incoming requests, spread out the posting rate to avoid flooding the account, and reduce the risk of duplicate tweets; second, it became apparent that a number of the patrons who were following us on Twitter had come to see this venue as their primary source of information on library services. Traditionally, notifications about items such as unexpected catalogue downtime would be broadcast as a banner across the top of every page of the library website. However, when server issues caused a weeklong series of interruptions to catalogue availability, Twitter users clamored for information about why they couldn't log-in—even though the banner had been up on the website since the problems began. We had created an expectation among these users that we would share important news and updates on Twitter in a timely manner, and now we needed to ensure that we were living up to this expectation. Twitter was no longer just an addition but one of our primary communication channels.

One of the advantages of using established social networking sites is that, as these have become an increasingly important part of the marketing and promotional landscape, a number of tools have been developed to help organizations manage them more effectively. We tested a few of these tools before settling on HootSuite as the best match for our needs. HootSuite provided us with the ability to post to multiple social networking accounts at the same time, meaning that we could share critical service updates across Twitter, Facebook, and other channels with one click; it allowed the assigning of incoming tweets to individual staff for follow-up; it eliminated the risk of duplicate tweets being submitted by different staff members; and it enabled us to schedule tweets, which proved a particular benefit in that we could space out the day's tweets evenly and avoid large gaps when the library was closed or no web team members were available.

The other advantage that HootSuite gave us was significantly improved metrics on how our Twitter feed was being used. We knew that our follower numbers held up impressively against other public libraries, but as a metric, follower count alone is a pretty blunt instrument; Twitter is full of spam accounts that automatically follow other accounts in an effort to boost their own numbers. An in-depth analysis of followers would provide more meaningful data about who is subscribed to the @VPL account, but this would be a considerably more time-consuming task. (While we have not yet conducted a full analysis, smaller-scale reviews of sample sets of followers indicate that @ VPL is doing well in this regard: followers are mainly individual Vancouverites, then local organizations and other libraries.) One of the most important metrics provided by HootSuite is the tracking of traffic to links that are shared using the ow.ly link shortener, which allows us to measure Twitter's ability to drive traffic back to the main VPL website.

Measuring the success of the account in a meaningful way is paramount, as it supports the work effort that we put into creating content and maintaining social networking accounts. We began by moving beyond follower count to examine retweets and feedback, monitoring the number of times that our followers forwarded our posts or submitted questions or direct responses to @VPL. As the tools have improved, our ability to probe and analyze the level of engagement that the account is achieving continues to grow. The excellent new Social-Biblio site (http://www.social-biblio.ca) allows us to measure the sentiment of tweets that mention @VPL, breaking user feedback into positive, negative, and neutral. Social-Biblio also allows us to track all the major metrics—followers, number of tweets, @VPL mentions, retweets—against 116 other Canadian public libraries that also use Twitter to communicate with their patrons.

Another new tool that is generating considerable interest among libraries is SocialFlow (http://www.socialflow.com), which analyzes the Twitter fan base for individual accounts and identifies topics that are of particular interest at certain times. Tweets that are entered ahead of time are then posted according to the topic that is most likely to resonate with the audience, not by a predetermined schedule. Organizations using SocialFlow, including the New York Public Library, report measurably increased engagement, and we look forward to exploring this and other possibilities as we continue to build our social media presence and reach more of our patrons with this content.

Formal acknowledgment of Twitter's importance as a communication channel for the library came in August 2010. A small-scale refresh of the home page (http://www.vpl.ca) was carried out, the first since the full-site redesign in 2008. Home page real estate is always the most hotly contested web property for any library, and VPL is no exception. As part of the refresh, a Twitter widget was placed on the home page so that @VPL's latest tweets would appear here as well as on the Twitter timeline (Figure 6.2).

POLICY AND GUIDELINES

With Twitter, Facebook, and other social media accounts firmly established as communication and content-sharing platforms for the library, the other important administrative piece that needed to be developed was a formal social media policy and guidelines for the organization. This meant treading a fine line between an undoubted need for structure and guidance and not putting in place so rigid a set of rules that the accounts would lose the spontaneity and freedom that make them such an effective and means of communicating news and engaging users.

As awareness of the VPL pilot accounts grew among staff and conferences and the professional literature began enthusiastically exploring the potential

Figure 6.2. Vancouver Public Library home page; Twitter feed, center left.

of these tools for libraries, individual librarians began taking the initiative to create accounts for their work areas. This led to variance in naming conventions, URL choice, and look and feel, unintentionally diminishing the impact of the VPL brand. The time and effort required to keep accounts refreshed with regular content was sometimes challenging, especially for smaller locations with fewer staff. It became clear that a central policy was needed to ensure consistency across accounts and provide clarity around posting expectations for account administrators.

As the policy took shape, we established that we needed to address three distinct areas:

- Guidelines for the setup, administration, and use of organizational accounts
- Terms of use for patron-generated content on VPL's web properties
- Policy for personal use of social media when self-identifying as a VPL employee

For the public terms of use, we largely followed the broader City of Vancouver policy, which was under development at the same time. The terms of use specify the types of content that the library considers inappropriate and that may be subject to removal if posted on a library account (these can be viewed online at https://www.vpl.ca/about/details/social_media_terms_of_use).

The policy for personal use of social media when self-identifying as a VPL employee was perhaps the hardest section to craft. VPL has more than 800 staff, many of whom use professional social networking sites such as LinkedIn or are actively involved in professional dialogue through personal blogs, listservs, or discussion groups. Many more have Facebook accounts where VPL is publicly listed as their employer. A delicate balance exists between protecting the organizational name and not discouraging or constraining staff from participating in professional dialogue. The policy makes it clear that such participation is not only welcome but encouraged, and it provides instruction on when staff should indicate that their views are their own and not necessarily representative of VPL.

For the web team, the section of the policy with the most impact on day-to-day work is the guidelines. These cover the following topics:

- Considerations for creating and managing a social media account
- Process for creating a new organizational account
- Central administration of accounts by the web team
- Naming conventions for accounts
- Content creation

Before beginning the process of setting up an account, staff are asked to consider the purpose and goals of the account and the workload that will be involved in making it successful. General standards are provided so that they can see exactly how often they would need to update a Twitter feed or Facebook page for the account to generate sufficient interest to get off the ground. Where staff feel there is a genuine need to establish a social media presence but insufficient time to support it, they are encouraged to submit their content requests to the web team to be broadcast on the main VPL accounts. This approach ensures that all branches and departments at the library can participate in VPL's social media activity, even if they do not have a separate account.

New account requests are approved by the manager or head of a particular department or branch and then submitted to the web team to set up. This ensures that naming conventions are followed, that web team members have administrative access to all accounts, and that all local administrators have been shown the guidelines and policy prior to taking the account over. This has streamlined the account creation process considerably and eliminated problems such as rogue naming conventions and orphan accounts being left inaccessible if the administrator leaves the library.

The last piece of the guidelines explains how to act as the voice of the library on its various social media accounts, including recommendations around the voice and tone of posts.

A number of branches have established very successful Facebook pages with a strong community focus but have not typically pursued Twitter as a communications platform. The Facebook pages can also be linked under the umbrella of the main VPL Facebook page, whereas Twitter accounts stand alone and run a higher risk of brand dilution if they become too diversified. A central e-mail account has been created where branches and work units can submit requests for posts on the main Twitter account, and web team members take turns monitoring this account and crafting and uploading the tweets. All social media account administrators are also added to a central listserv and strongly encouraged to share ideas with one another.

NEXT STEPS

With the creation of a new digital services department and an overarching digital services strategy imminent, it's an exciting time for social media at VPL. While our approach to these tools has evolved from side-of-the-desk pilots to organized, strategic, and measured management over the past few years, opportunities still exist to tie our use of social media more closely to our overall organizational priorities and integrate them more closely with existing marketing workflows.

New analysis tools will allow us to examine the nature of our audience more closely and better determine the effectiveness and resonance of the content we post. VPL has 275,000 registered cardholders, and the 13,000 users of our various social media accounts (Twitter, Facebook, Flickr, YouTube, and Pinterest) represent approximately 5% of this number. While our follower numbers have increased rapidly over time and compare well to other libraries of a similar size, considerable scope exists to grow our existing audience and increase our reach to patrons through social media.

One of the challenges of working with third-party tools and websites is that it is hard to be certain how long the existing services of the moment will last (remember when MySpace was the hottest thing on the web?) or what new killer apps might rise up to replace or stand alongside them (see the current wave of Pinterest pilots). For a long time, our social media mantra was "responsive, not reactive"; our goal was to position ourselves in such a way that we were able to pilot and evaluate new tools quickly without wasting valuable time and resources by simply jumping on every passing bandwagon. Ideally, the future will see us moving from responsive to proactive, identifying potential even earlier in the game and targeting our efforts more effectively. We also need to remain mindful that many of these tools do have a limited shelf life, and when the community moves on, we must be prepared to let go and move along with it.

The most important lesson that we have learned in the past 4 years is that there absolutely is a place for the library on the social network. The key word here is *social*; these online gathering spaces are ones that the community has chosen, and in them we can find an active, vocal group of users who are keen to hear what we have to say and give us their feedback. With a strategic approach that combines the right amounts of structure and flexibility, these tools create powerful engagement opportunities and a very different image of the library in the eyes of those who use them.

7

Successful Blogging Strategy and Design

Jason Paul Michel
Miami University Libraries

Blogging is certainly nothing new. Done right, however, a blog can serve as a rich medium through which users can continually discover new materials, new services, and new reasons to maintain their relationship with your library.

This chapter considers the Miami University Libraries' News and Notes blog as a springboard to discuss how to implement and maintain a successful blog strategy as a conduit of information and library discovery. Specifically, it discusses content and content creators (having an abundance of both is key), technological considerations (including feeding blog content to several social medias for maximum reach and efficient use of staff time), resource considerations, user response and assessment tools, and future possibilities.

WHEN AND WHY

In late 2007, the Miami University Libraries convened a Social Networking Working Group. The group's charge was to discover and examine emerging social web technologies and trends and work to create new library services and tools to take advantage of those technologies as well as understand these new communication and information-seeking methods to shape services to fit those methods. One of the many projects that came out of this group's work was to initiate a library blog, as many libraries were beginning to do at the time.

Before implementing the blog idea, we needed to convince our colleagues of the importance of blogging in addition to the other social media ideas that we believed it necessary to explore. No social media or blogging endeavor will succeed without buy-in from a critical mass of librarians. To have a rich and dynamic social media platform, many people need to contribute on a consistent basis.

So to persuade our colleagues, we asked ourselves "Why?" The reasons that follow encapsulate our thinking and provide a philosophical foundation for our proposals. First, the library's greatest strength is its people. These tools will better highlight, utilize, and optimize this strength. They will put a face on library services. Second, our users are interacting and communicating in new ways. We must understand and use these new communication mediums. The popularity of social networking is rising at an extremely rapid rate. We believe that, though individual applications may come and go, the idea of social software is here to stay.

The experimental SOLR-ized catalog will feature all of the classic social software features, such as tagging and bookmarking. If our catalog is experimenting with these ideas, it only makes sense that our public services do as well. Learning models are evolving. Collaboration and active learning are gaining in importance, as opposed to passive learning styles. Librarians can serve as facilitators of collaboration and communication. One of the predominant ideas of these tools is one of play, experimentation, and perpetual beta. We can't be afraid of trying these tools. Finally, perception is critical. Nearly all of the most highly used websites feature social software aspects: RSS, ratings, reviews, tagging (folksonomies), comments, friends or contacts, profiles, and so on. Users who view our site may be less inclined to use it merely because it lacks these qualities. On the flip side, users that see that we are using these tools may be more inclined to use our resources and approach librarians with questions.

We were able to convince enough librarians to form an active pool of blog contributors, and throughout the next year, we worked diligently to expand on the blog idea as an outreach tool and develop it into a medium to actively promote the library. We put this idea into place by crafting a loose set of subject ideas intended to guide and inspire the bloggers, designing the blog template, workflow procedures, and the interface design on the library's home page. The chief objectives of the library blog were to promote and unearth library materials and collections, highlight and market our varied services, celebrate staff and library achievements, and develop a personal relationship with our users.

BLOG CONTRIBUTORS AND CONTENT

From the inception, it was determined that it should be a multicontributor blog. Laying responsibility of producing a rich and dynamic blog on the shoulders of one person is inefficient and will ultimately lead to a paucity of content. We decided to invite all of our public service librarians to contribute to the blog. To ensure quality and appropriateness of the blog content, we did put some editorial control mechanisms in place. Essentially, any public service librarian had the freedom to blog, but the ultimate publication of the post was up to the discretion of the user experience librarian in charge of the overall blog project.

Knowing that we would need several people contributing to the blog, we knew that we must grease the wheels, so to speak, in terms of content. Asking colleagues to just blog about "whatever" doesn't help and can lead to blog posts that miss our strategic mark. So, we devised a set of subjects and themes that contributors could blog about. This took the burden off of them to come up with ideas.

The initial set of subjects came about through a thorough brainstorming session and was later added to by interested bloggers. The current list of subjects is the following:

New materials: Bloggers write blog posts about new materials under their purview. New books, videos, reference materials, and so on that are within their subject areas are easy targets for valuable blog posts.

Digital videos: Occasionally, the library produces video tutorials or other video-based content. These blog posts direct users to this material.

Branch and department news: There is always something happening in individual departments: whether it is new materials arriving, new databases added, departmental changes, or new initiatives. Share this information with your users. Social media is all about parting the curtain on previously hidden information.

Current events: This is one of the most popular blogging subjects. What we encourage our bloggers to do is take a look at what is happening in the world at large or in your area of expertise and write a blog post about it. We also encourage bloggers to tie our resources with those current events. One of our bloggers writes posts about the annual writing awards and long write-ups of authors who have passed away. This allows us to celebrate the lives and achievements of writers and give our readers direct access to their works.

Campus and community events: This subject gives us another opportunity to showcase our services and resources. Let's say, for example, there is an LGBT (lesbian, gay, bisexual, transgender) parade occurring on campus. A blogger can write about the upcoming parade and suggest some books, videos, and other resources to further enlighten our readers.

Digital collections: Unique collections in every library are usually very rich with interesting content. Handpicking individual images or a set of images and writing a blog post about the content of the images is an easy post to write and interesting for readers.

Library events: Write rich blog posts about upcoming library events. Each year, our library hosts the African American Read-In and the Women's Read-In. This gives us the opportunity to not only inform our users of these great events but also write about great writers and some of their works that we have in our collections.

Miami history: Our library, like most libraries, has a very rich institutional archive. Material from this archive can be blogged about extensively. The most fruitful time to write these types of posts is around notable institutional anniversaries.

Multimedia picks: One resource that often gets overlooked is our library's multimedia resources. Many users don't realize the breadth of a library's multimedia collection. Writing blog posts that highlight these collections is a good way to get the word out. One example would be to write a post about the horror films in your collection during Halloween.

Staff: The heart of any organization is the staff. These are the people that make everything happen. One of the primary aspects of social media is that it gives users a behind-the-scenes look at things and personalizes what were once faceless entities. Write blog posts about your staff members' achievements, publications, and the like. Or just write a bio of each staff member, listing his or her expertise, interests, and more.

Technology: Whenever your library embarks on a new technology or offers a new digital service, write a blog post about it.

It is very important to create a set of subjects as in the aforementioned list. While some categories may not prove as rich as others, it really helps guide and inspire the blog contributors. Without a loose set of categories, contributors may feel indecisive about what to write about. Whatever subject categories you decide on for your blog, make sure that it is devised with as much input from the staff as possible.

TECHNICAL SETUP—BLOG AND SOCIAL MEDIA LINKAGE

We utilize the Drupal content management system for our website. Drupal is an open-source web development infrastructure made up of various "modules." Drupal comes with a handful of core modules. Designers build on these core modules with additional, community-designed modules.

The News and Notes blog is designed using the Blog, Taxonomy, and User core modules. These modules come with the default installation of Drupal.

We also installed the Views module, a noncore module that helped with the construction of the blog infrastructure. I discuss the role of each module individually and delineate how they all fit together.

The Blog module is a core Drupal module that comes standard out of the box. While it is a core module, it is technically optional and thus must be enabled prior to using. To enable the Blog module on your Drupal installation, go to *sitename*/admin/build/modules/list and check the "Enabled" box next to "Blog."

The initial setup for the Blog module allows users with the proper permissions to give a blog post a title and the body of the post. The blogging interface does by default not come with a WYSIWYG editor, so any links or images must be added via HTML tags. Any further additions, such as tags or categories, must be added with further modules which I will discuss below.

As the administrator of a Drupal site, you have control over what your users can and cannot do on the site. This is achieved through the User module, specifically the Permissions and Roles functionalities. When managing a website that is used by multiple constituencies, it is important to be able to set up varying levels of permissions based on the users' role on the site. For our blog, we identified public service librarians who were interested in writing blog posts. For these users, we created a role of "Blogger." To create and edit roles on your Drupal site, go to *sitename*/admin/user/roles.

For each role in your Drupal site, you can bestow certain permissions to interact with each module in very finely controlled ways. To allow the people that we recognized as Bloggers to write and edit blog posts, we needed to give them the proper permissions. This can be done at *sitename*/admin/user/permissions. For the Blog module, the choices for permissions are as follows: create blog entries; delete any blog entry; delete own blog entries; edit any blog entry; and edit own blog entries. To bestow each permission, admins must merely check them off.

Another element in the blog construction is the use of Drupal taxonomies. Taxonomy is an optional core Drupal module like the Blog module. We used taxonomy to achieve two things: first, to give bloggers a controlled vocabulary of tags to apply to each blog post and, second, to control which blog posts get published to the main blog, viewable from the home page of the website. Drupal admin users have the ability to create taxonomies and taxonomy terms under each. For the blog, we created a taxonomy called "NN Categories," with NN being short for News and Notes. This taxonomy contained several terms, such as "Current Events," "New Materials," and "Digital Collections," from which the bloggers can choose to apply to their blog posts.

The final module that ties everything together is Views. This is not a core module, but it can be added to your Drupal installation. Views can be found at http://drupal.org/project/views. The Views module allows you to create dynamic custom webpages within your primary site. The page for our blog, http://www.lib.muohio.edu/news_and_notes, is achieved through the use of the Views module, which gives you full control over what is displayed on the page. This is the editorial control that is needed to ensure that erroneous, misleading, or inappropriate blog content is not posted to the primary blog view.

The two primary elements in Views are Content and Filters. Essentially using these two elements, we can build from the bottom up a webpage with the exact content we want, in the exact order we want, with the proper filters and sort order. So, in the case of the News and Notes view, we chose blog title, blog author, taxonomy terms, and blog text. If you wanted to build a view that just listed the blog titles and not the actual text of the blog, you could do that, too. The Views module allows you to be extremely detailed in the content you pick to display.

So we have the content that we want to display, but we need to put some filters on it. To get an idea of what is meant by filters, we chose the following filters for the News and Notes view. The first filter is that the type of content must be a blog entry; the second is that it be published; and the final filter is that the taxonomy term "News and Notes" be applied. This final filter here is what gives us control over what is finally published.

Before being posted to the News and Notes page, the content must go through these filters. If a blog entry is written but not published, it won't get through to the main page. If a blog entry is written and published but does not contain the taxonomy term "News and Notes," it won't get through to the main page. We have one editor on staff who has final say over what gets pushed to the main site, and that person is the only one with permission to apply the taxonomy term "News and Notes." So, that person reads the potential blog posts and, if everything is okay, applies the taxonomy term, which passes through all the filters and is published to the main site.

SOCIAL MEDIA SYNDICATION

Once you have settled on the type of content that your bloggers will write about and have set up the technical infrastructure of the blog, you may think that you've finished the job. But you haven't quite yet. Of critical importance is to disseminate your blog content as widely as possible. You cannot assume that users are going to come to your site to view your content. In fact, you can assume they won't. You must get your content out via social media channels. Fortunately, this can be done in an automated way, further maximizing both blog content reach and staff time.

All blogging platforms will have RSS options, and Drupal is no exception. To syndicate your blog content, you must have access to its RSS feed. We used a web service called dlvr.it to automatically post the News and Notes content to both our Twitter and Facebook accounts. Dlvr.it is a great syndication tool, as it gives you a great deal of control over how your content is fed out to different sites. Dlvr.it refers to each syndication as a *route*. The first element you'll need to set up a route via dlvr.it is the RSS feed URL for your blog. Once you've entered the RSS URL and dlvr.it has verified its authenticity, then you can edit some of the finer details of the route.

The first detail that you can control is how often dlvr.it checks your feed for new updates. If you have a very active blog, you can have dlvr.it check your feed every 15 minutes or less, or you can check it once a day for a less active blog. Dlvr.it refers to this as a "feed update period." Having decided on this time, you can then indicate how many items are posted during that time. Again, if you have a very active blog, you could indicate that you'd like dlvr.it to send only two blog posts every 15 minutes. This level of control will help you ensure that you're not inundating your Twitter or Facebook followers with blog posts all at once. Rather, you can space out your content over a wider period.

In addition to determining how often your feed is checked for content, you can set up a scheduled time or window that your content is sent along to your social media accounts. The URL-shortening service bit.ly released data about the best times to post social media content. The results of its research can be found at http://bit.ly/PGMWKZ. It is a good idea to configure your dlvr. it account to send your blog content during these times for maximal impact. Further configuration is available, including advanced filtering options and the ability to apply prefixed text to your tweets and Facebook posts.

The next step is to set up your destinations. Dlvr.it gives you the ability to send content to Twitter, Facebook, LinkedIn, Tumblr, and Del.icio.us. All that you need to do is enter your account detail, and you are all set up and ready to go. Keep in mind that the more access points to your content, the higher the probability that it will be seen. Getting into and remaining in our users' consciousness should be a goal of all libraries.

STAFF BUY-IN AND OTHER RESOURCES

For any blog to have a chance at success, it must be dynamic and continually updated. Your content is competing for the mindspace of a user base who is consuming content from dozens, hundreds, or even thousands of other content providers. If your blog is updated a couple of times a week, chances are high that it will be missed or buried by the constant flood of information.

Because of this reality, it is critical that as many librarians and suitable staff personnel as possible are contributing to the content of the blog. Any developer of a blogging program must stress this to achieve as much staff buy-in as possible. Barring including blog writing in the job description of all librarians, the only way to achieve staff buy-in is through spirited enthusiasm. We were able to sell the importance of the blog to enough of our librarians to form a core group of bloggers who write interesting posts and help us maintain our visibility to our users.

The first significant outlay of time dedicated to this blog project was the development of the Drupal blog infrastructure as previously delineated. This took the lead developer roughly 20 hours of time to set up. This does not include the time spent to set up the Drupal content management system, which was a wholly separate project involving many staff members. It is certainly not necessary to develop a custom blog in Drupal or any other content management system. The most efficient use of time would be to set up a blog using a blogging platform such as WordPress or Blogger. Developing a blog with this strategy will take less time and less web programming expertise.

In addition to the initial outlay of time by the lead developer, bloggers typically spend an average of 20 to 30 minutes per week writing their posts. This is a minimal investment in time. Coupling this small amount of time with the wide dissemination of the content via the dlvr.it system makes it clear that this is an efficient use of staff time.

Our web team utilizes Google analytics to analyze the traffic on our site. Since its inception, our blog averages around 500 views per month, thanks in large part to traffic coming to it via our Facebook and Twitter accounts. In addition to that number, it seems that the blog has an effect on book circulation as well. A limited examination of some of our popular blog posts, such as the post about *Downton Abbey* and the *Hunger Games*, indicates that the majority of the books mentioned in the blog had checkout dates after the blog posting. We cannot claim causation here, but it is interesting and worth a detailed study.

We intend on further strengthening our blogging platform by pursuing the following initiatives. First, we will assign a lead blogger for each department or branch library. This person will seek out blog stories and serve as the primary proofreader for his or her department's content. Second, we will automate our statistical tracking workflow so that bloggers are continually updated about the reach and popularity of their posts, serving as an ongoing motivator. Finally, we will continually work to change the work culture to one that views sharing content and behind-the-scenes information as an integral part of our mission. Blogging will then not be seen as something that we should probably do after everything else is done; rather, it will be seen as something that is done as an integral part of our work.

Based on several years of this blog program, there are a few things that we should have implemented from the start. Here are a few pieces of advice that will help with the success of your blog project.

1. Strongly advocate for the codification of blog writing as a core responsibility of all librarians. It need not be an unwieldy amount of work, maybe a blog post a week or month. This will guarantee that the blog has the amount of content it needs to remain fresh and relevant. If this is not possible, it is critical that you strongly encourage as many people in your organization as possible to contribute to the success of the blog.
2. Assign the role of blog editor to one staff person. This person will be responsible for seeking out potential stories and coming up with the ideas for blog postings. In addition to that, she or he could ask other staff members to write certain blog posts about topics they know. This blog editor would also proofread and judge each blog post for suitability and appropriateness prior to publication.
3. Choose software that is simple to use. The goal of the blog is to have high-quality content on a consistent basis, and any technological barriers that may stand in the way of this goal should be avoided. The simpler the blogging platform, the better.
4. Make weekly or monthly goals and stick to them. At the bare minimum, your blog should have at least one posting per day, and the ideal blog would have several. Again, your content is competing for the mindspace of users who are consuming content from dozens or hundreds of other blogs and information providers, so the more content, the better.
5. Utilize an analytics or statistics tracker. This will allow you to see how many hits your blog posts are getting, which will help you determine the type of post that is appealing to your readers, allowing you to further hone the voice of your blog. Inform the blog writers of the number of page views to encourage them to write more.

8

Social Catalogs: Implementing an Online Social Community as an Extension to Our Physical Libraries

LAUREL TARULLI

Dalhousie University

It's exciting news when we finally get the go-ahead from our management team or library board to explore the development of a new service or the acquisition of new software. For many of us, it may be a once-in-a-career opportunity to develop or implement an innovative service that changes the path of our libraries. Most often, this is the result of sharing resources and attempts by management to allow each area of library service a "kick at the can" opportunity, and when our time comes to take charge and work on an exciting project, we want to be prepared and armed with as much knowledge as possible to make it a success. In fact, the opportunity to implement a project or lead a team in creating a new service often begins months, if not years, before the opportunity actually presents itself. While we prepare for our "kick at the can," we can start visualizing the service we'd like to enhance or the tools we'd like to implement, recognizing the need in our library for this enhancement. With the rise of social media and social tools in an "I want it now" society, many of the projects that we are developing and implementing revolve around the need to reach users whenever and wherever they are—in essence, extending the library beyond its physical walls and into a social space where connections, interactions, and information are limitless. With that idea in mind, one naturally has to consider the library catalog as a potential platform for creating an online community of users, with their interactions revolving around readers' services, the collection, and programming.

This chapter examines how one library implemented an overlay on top of its existing library catalog. While the technical term for an overlay is often called a *discovery tool overlay*, many professionals simply use the generic term *social catalog*. Social catalogs are seen as interactive and dynamic catalogs that are more user friendly and intuitive while offering features that existing (classic) catalogs don't. These social features include tagging, rating, reviewing, interacting with staff or other users, creating user lists, and sharing items from within the catalog. Ideally, it's a social online community that provides a gateway to information and people. In this case, the social catalog implemented is AquaBrowser.

BACKGROUND AND PREPARATION

Well over a year before the soft launch of the new social catalog occurred, Halifax Public Libraries in Halifax, Nova Scotia, decided to explore the idea of implementing an overlay on top of their existing online public access catalog. While not ready to replace the entire integrated library system (ILS) due to the many components that are interlinked with the catalog, including circulation and collection development, management recognized the need to address the shortcomings of the outdated interface and lack of features in the library catalog that patrons expected and, in fact, were taking for granted on almost every commercial site, online bookstore, and social networking site. But how do you go about deciding what catalog overlay is right for your library, and how do you sell the idea to staff and patrons?

A team of librarians and managers was created to act as liaisons and representatives for staff in the decision-making and purchasing process. This was an essential element that resulted in identifying key members of the system who had an interest in social technology or an expertise of a strong service within the library that would likely benefit greatly from the implementation of a social catalog. Once this team was created, it had to learn about the various vendors who provided social catalogs and their features. This was an interesting time, as many of the team members were not familiar with social catalogs.

Let's start with examining how Halifax Public Libraries went about deciding which catalog overlay would best meet their needs, including staff and patron expectations as well as budgetary restrictions. There were five key steps taken in the selection process and purchase of a social catalog:

Step 1: Identifying what other libraries are doing.
Step 2: Research.
Step 3: Consideration of the following factors:
- Proprietary versus open-source software
- Solution requirements
- Identifying user needs and groups
- Budget, staff resources, and timeline for implementation

Step 4: Vendor presentations.
Step 5: Speaking with colleagues at other libraries about their experiences and opinions.

Even a team well acquainted with social catalogs and their features should take the opportunity to examine and experience what other libraries have successfully (or not so successfully) implemented. Each team member was charged with exploring other libraries' catalogs. These included catalogs that were both overlays and full replacements of existing ILSs. The reason was to experience and gather knowledge of the wide variety of elements, layouts, and features that are possible. It was also an opportunity to familiarize the team with the many vendors providing these catalogs and the features that were unique to each vendor or were common among all vendors' products.

While the team was familiarizing itself with various catalog platforms, the cataloging librarian—a position I held at the time—was charged with researching these products and finding out about their strengths and weaknesses. In essence, I was looking for reviews of these catalogs, product comparisons, professional opinions, and research articles that may have examined these catalogs in further depth. For example, had any research been conducted examining the success of social features in library catalogs?

The research provided an interesting glimpse into these new library catalogs. While vendors promised an "if you build it, they will come" outcome, there is no research supporting this claim. And if vendors' assessments of their products were conducted, they remain unavailable to libraries. However, blog posts and professional journals did provide an interesting and realistic glimpse into the implementation of social catalogs and reflections on the process.

Armed with the information that we gleaned from research and our familiarity with various products available to libraries, the team at Halifax Public Libraries was able to move forward in discussing the issues of proprietary software versus open-source software, creating wish lists and must-have lists for features and functions, identifying the various new and existing user groups who will benefit as well as struggle with these features, and defining the limitations of budget, staff resources, and timelines for accomplishing the implementation and bringing the catalog into fruition. This phase allowed the team to pinpoint elements that were required for the purchase of a catalog overlay and identify vendors whose social catalogs appeared to be a good fit with these requirements.

Once vendors were identified, they were asked to provide a presentation of their product for the team. This allowed the team to bring in additional colleagues to view the products as well as ask questions about features and glimpse some additional behind-the-scenes functionality and interoperability. After the presentation, it was requested that the vendors provide sample responses to a request for proposal (RFP). This provided the team with an understanding of what the RFPs would look like when received "formally" and what type of information they can ask for, wish for, demand, or change. The various vendors were also asked about special customization features, including features unique to their product, and questioned on outstanding concerns from the team, such as a response to a negative review by another library using their product.

The final step in this process was to contact other libraries for their candid opinions on the implementation and overall success of their social catalogs. For example, it was helpful having discussions with libraries using the same ILS or with the same amount of resources. In addition, learning firsthand about the implementation process, problems that arose, and lessons learned was extremely enlightening from someone who wasn't selling the product.

As these steps were slowly traveled through, the local expertise grew, and the team at Halifax Public Libraries felt as though it were finally in a position to extend RFPs to several social catalog vendors.

OBJECTIVES

What is the purpose of implementing a social catalog? It's easy to rattle off the common excuses for any new service. "Patrons expect it." "We'll attract more users." "Our catalog will be able to compete with commercial sites." Whatever the typical response, the objectives need to be clear and grounded in a firm foundation. Understanding the various products is essential to addressing concrete objectives that go beyond providing a lipstick and makeup enhancement to the library catalog.

The main objective of this project was to provide enhanced user access to library collections and provide a single access point for library information. In essence, creating a localized Google that brings together library collections, programs, local interests, and the community by giving users a more intuitive interface and a means of interacting with the library through social features. One can think of it as a gateway used to access information, rather than a destination spot.

When Halifax Public Libraries were exploring the possibility of purchasing a social catalog, various key managers within the library system were asked to compile a wish list of functions and features, as well as a must-have list. The cataloging department was asked to do the same.

Compiling these lists is not a simple task. While it's easy to list all of the features we'd like, many professionals not familiar with social catalogs listed features found on commercial websites, features found on library websites with custom-made ILSs, or functions that are unavailable or not possible when implementing an overlay that pulls information from existing content sources within the catalog component of the ILS or from identified sources from external websites. However, every idea and item listed by staff were considered. Some were extremely helpful, some obvious, and yet others enlightening and creative. All of the librarians and managers who submitted these "need and wants" lists contributed to the process and ultimately to the three lists that were created: must-haves, must-have in the future, and wish list. All of the vendors invited to respond to the RFP were provided with these lists to address. A list of the key mandatory requirements was as follows:

- Faceted navigation
- Library-defined relevancy ranking
- Sing search research screen that included a Google-like search box, set of related terms, relevancy-ranked results, and a faceted browsing capability for further refinement based on library-selected criteria
- Close to real-time synchronization with ILS database
- Indexing that is unattended and automated
- Single sign-on
- Ability to display enriched content, such as cover art, table of contents, and reviews
- In-house ability to customize, define, and make changes to interface and design components

There were also social elements that were vital to the adoption and implementation of a social catalog:

- The ability to add and search tags
- Creation of personal and public lists
- Searchable lists and users
- Creation of reviews
- Contribution of ratings

The final lists were based on the goals and objectives set forth by the library. If an item was desirable but didn't necessarily meet the present objectives, it was put on a wish list.

In the end, Halifax Public Libraries decided to purchase AquaBrowser, a social discovery tool provided by SerialSolutions.

IMPLEMENTATION AND RESOURCES

Many would think that placing an overlay over an existing catalog rather than replacing the entire software/database (ILS) would be easier. It may be. But implementing an overlay is not simple. Our traditional ILSs are bulky and full of components and content that differ from one vendor's ILS to another's. As a result, taking on the project of implementing a social catalog (in this case, a catalog overlay) requires in-house expertise in cataloging—in particular, at least one professional who is well versed in MARC coding and fields that dictate or display specific sources of information. A strong cataloging department also helps but is not critical. Also needed is an information technology team that understands the library's ILS intimately and a vendor support team that is available and willing to work with the library implementing the software on an almost-daily basis during installation.

There are two key elements to this implementation phase that make this clear. The first was in providing configuration sheets for every database, which required information extraction from within our existing ILS for display in the social catalog interface. As an overlay, AquaBrowser "fishes" information out of databases such as the catalog, extracting and organizing this information for display on its interface. As a result, every data source that needed to be displayed in AquaBrowser had to be reviewed. Pouring over the structure of MARC records within Halifax Public Libraries' ILS system Horizon, the cataloging team was required to determine which MARC fields were standard and used in every record, which fields varied, which fields were more important than others, and if there were unique fields to each record that would help extract and sort them in the overlay. Other configuration details included identifying the specific codes for every collection, every library branch, and media format. Once that was done, there were MARC subfields to be addressed. It would not be an exaggeration to say that even the examples just provided didn't scratch the service to the types of minute details required to be analyzed prior to being able to move forward with implementation.

With a strong information technology team, other technology issues can be addressed, such as security and privacy issues, compatibility, and memory/storage within the library server. For example, AquaBrowser needs to access a library's ILS remotely to export and then import all of the existing records. It does this to capture any changes made to records, add new cataloged records, and delete any old records. For this to happen, the information technology team needs to allow an outside source access past the firewall and provide enough memory so that the catalog continues to work for users while this extraction and importation occur.

There are several key factors that make implementation success. They include the accuracy and quality of the library's bibliographic records, knowledge of the existing ILS and how it works, and developing an excellent working relationship with your social catalog vendor implementation contact. While the last two points may seem obvious, the first point must be explored in case you're asking yourself why the quality of cataloging records is so important. The simple fact is that an overlay extracts identified information from existing library sources—specifically, the library catalog. With more results returned and organized, errors in records or a lack of uniformity becomes glaringly obvious. For example, if an author's name is not uniform and some have been entered with birth dates, birth and death dates, or no dates, the faceted navigation feature pulls up three sets of results for the same author. In other cases, if a subject heading is spelled incorrectly, the title attached to that record may not be included in results. One of the most obvious errors is incorrectly providing the correct format indicator. DVDs were being displayed as books formats, and kits were showing up as movies! As you can imagine, a significant amount of time within the cataloging department is required to clean up these records.

While the "backroom" work of implementing the new social catalog was underway, a lengthy "marketing" campaign began within the library to "sell" the idea of a social catalog to staff and to educate them on the many ways that a social catalog can be used (to enhance readers' services, collection development, young adult services, as well as promote library events such as author readings and book clubs). A tutorial was developed for this purpose, and the cataloging librarian and manager attended various meetings throughout the system to promote the idea of a new catalog and its key features.

THE LAUNCH

Prior to the staff beta launch in the early winter of 2009–2010, a tutorial (http://laureltarulli.wordpress.com/2010/12/07/online-aquabrowser-tutorial/) of the implemented social catalog AquaBrowser was created for all staff and for use as a resource manual in the coming months. Created in-house, this tutorial provides an overview of AquaBrowser, its basic use (how most users will want to use it), and a variety of ways to use the social features from a staff-side perspective—in essence, answering the question "How will this catalog benefit or enhance my area of service to patrons?" While met with varying degrees of success, it did provide many staff with their first glimpse at the new social catalog and how it works.

Approximately 6 months after the tutorial was first provided to staff, Halifax Public Libraries beta-launched AquaBrowser to the public on April 20, 2010. Rather than calling the social catalog by its vendor name AquaBrowser, the communications and marketing team branded the new catalog "Discover." A play on the fact that it's a discovery tool, it ties into Halifax Public Libraries' mission statement, which includes "Connecting people, enriching communities, inspiring discovery." Accordingly, the library viewed this new catalog not just as a static inventory that allows users to rate and write reviews but as a discovery tool. The discovery experience provides users with the opportunity to find what they are looking for, as well as to navigate through various tools to "discover" new items within the catalog and within the community. One of the most exciting features is the ability to search a topic and be provided with community group information and volunteer information around the city. These results sit side by side with books and DVDs within the library collection. Being able to pull the resources together and provide results that extend beyond the physical walls of the library and its collection excited all of our users—patrons and staff. The implementation team hoped that this branding and the enhanced features it provided not only met the original objectives but would exceed staff and patrons' expectations.

This beta launch provided an option for staff and patrons to continue to use the old catalog or choose to try out the new catalog. This allowed all of our users to ease into the idea of a social catalog and become accustomed to the new look and feel of an interactive and dynamic interface. Within days, the implementation team at the library were receiving feedback, both positive and negative. However, one patron's comments certainly let the staff know that social catalogs were on the right path to answering the needs and expectations of users:

> If one enjoys books, it can only be described as a positive addiction. I found the new catalogue very user friendly and easy on the eyes—i.e., not too busy. It is fun to use and easy to navigate and find search items. I particularly enjoyed the "Discovery" area on the left side of the screen.

Just under a year after the beta launch, the official launch of Discover at Halifax Public Libraries took place on March 1, 2011. Before the launch, public service staff were provided with professional training sessions by the implementation project leader at AquaBrowser. This allowed staff to become even more familiar with the catalog, and it provided yet another opportunity to ask questions or dig deeper into the functions of the catalog while being guided by an expert. By the time of the official launch, the new catalog had been improved on and customized to reflect a year's worth of feedback and branding. And staff were comfortable and familiar with the functions and features of the catalog. The communications and marketing department played a large role in the official launch of the catalog, promoting the idea of Discover, creating buttons, flyers, ad campaigns, T-shirts, lanyards, and so on. Staff were encouraged to promote the new catalog and provide assistance and tips for patrons on how to use it in ways that best fit their needs or wants. While the campaign slowly died a natural death as patrons and staff become more familiar and comfortable with Discover, staff still wear lanyards identifying themselves as staff that use and promote the Discover brand.

ASSESSMENT

When the beta version of Discover was launched to the public, it was provided with an opportunity to voice its opinions on the new catalog. A survey was provided online, offering patrons an invitation to provide feedback to management. For most of the questions, there were three choices for a response: *useful, not useful, didn't notice.* The questions were broken down into the following categories:

- What patrons thought of each feature (the feature was listed, asking for one of the three responses)
- If the features were hard or easy to use
- Catalog preference (new social catalog or existing classic catalog)
- Additional comments for the features and ease of use
- Request for e-mail, gender, and age group and if the patron would be willing to provide follow-up feedback if contacted

The feedback received from this survey, while self-selecting by nature, was helpful to staff. It allowed staff to identify patron groups who were most likely going to be resistant to the new catalog, as well as concerns or compliments that allowed for improvement or reinforced existing opinions. The survey was available throughout the beta phase.

Also important to the development of the catalog were the focus groups that were held. Interestingly, the purpose of these focus groups was not only to invite existing users but to reach nonlibrary users. These focus groups invited comment and discussion after a live demonstration. This allowed staff to roll out the Discover brand, introduce the key functions and features, and market the objectives for implementing a social catalog. After the presentation, focus group attendees were asked to fill out a short form for additional information.

The majority of formal and informal assessments took place at the front end of implementation. From asking staff for their must-have lists and wish lists to holding focus groups and providing an online survey, the strongest focus for assessing the new catalog was front-heavy. It is to be expected in a lengthy and expensive project that a significant amount of resources are used to provide enough evidence and feedback to support a new and successful initiative.

After the official launch, staff and patrons alike were encouraged to continue to provide feedback. In fact, they continue to do so, which allows staff to address or enhance the new catalog. However, there are no plans to formally assess the new catalog or create benchmark assessments.

During the year that Discover was in its public beta phase, there was an additional, external resource examining the use of social catalogs. With the assistance of an OCLC research grant, Dr. Louise Spiteri and I conducted a transaction log analysis of two libraries in Canada: Edmonton Public Library and Halifax Public Libraries. Transaction log analysis is a way of collecting data unobtrusively without directly interfacing with the catalog users, and it allows researchers to observe and analyze user behaviors. After a preliminary review of the literature, we noted that while the social catalog had been in use for over 5 years in Canada and the United States, the actual value of social features of these catalogs, such as tags, reviews, and ratings to the end user, had not been examined.

Transaction log analysis was used to answer the following research questions:

- How do public library users interact with social discovery systems? Specifically, which enhanced catalog features do they use (e.g., faceted navigation, user-contributed content such as tagging, reviews, and ratings, and with which frequency)?
- How does usage between the two social discovery systems compare? Specifically, are there commonalities or differences between how public library users use the enhanced catalog features of the two social discovery systems?

Most existing usability studies provide important insight into how people interact with online catalogs and how these experiences can be improved; what becomes evident from these studies is that catalogs should reflect the information needs and terminology of users, rather than library staff. With one exception, these usability studies focus on only the traditional model of the catalog or library website, where content is controlled by library staff.

The results of our analysis suggest that the patrons and staff at both Edmonton and Halifax are making limited use of the social features found in social catalogs that allow them to interact with the catalog records and with one another. An important question to consider is the extent to which people are motivated to add tags, reviews, or ratings to an item after they have read, seen, or listened to it. Since the implementation and maintenance of social catalogs are costly, it is important for library management to make informed decisions about which system features are the most cost-effective and how these features may be better tailored to meet user needs. A noticeable limitation of transaction log analysis is that it does not tell us why patrons use these features and, perhaps more important, why they do not. As a result, even if public libraries are unable due to lack of resources or unwilling to conduct a formal analysis of the implementation of their social catalogs, future research needs to focus on users' motivations for engaging with the social features of social catalogs and their perceptions of and satisfaction with the benefits of these features.

ADVICE TO OTHER PROFESSIONALS

Halifax Public Libraries continue to implement additional features in Discover and continually attempt to address the informal feedback received from public service staff with ongoing enhancements. Discover is not viewed as an implemented piece of technology with a completion date but as an ongoing, living organism that is always evolving. Understanding that these new catalogs are not static but require ongoing assessments enhancements will aid in the success that the catalog enjoys among staff and patrons.

While the overall implementation of Discover was lengthy and required a significant amount of buy-in and expertise, it is viewed as a success. Indeed, AquaBrowser uses Halifax Public Libraries' catalog as an example on its website. But with all projects, those who participated in its implementation experienced many emotions, including frustration, excitement, uncertainty, and curiosity (to name just a few!).

For any library wishing to implement a social catalog, there are several key points that should be explored before moving forward. While many have already been discussed in this chapter, there are several additional areas that should be identified:

- Think outside the box. Social tools within the libraries will not be used the same way that they are on Amazon or LibraryThing. What motivates patrons to use these tools? Consideration needs to be given to how and why we want these tools. Perhaps we are just using the tools the wrong way and for the wrong purposes.
- Understand that poor cataloging and inconsistencies within cataloging practices will become obvious with the implementation of these catalogs.

Be prepared to defend the amount of time it will take to correct these shortcomings (and why they exist).

- Become familiar with all of the social catalogs available and delve into their shortcomings.
- Explore the option of smartphone platforms and other handheld devices immediately. What options are available? Are different vendors compatible with the product? While the vendor of a catalog overlay may provide a mobile option, many underlying ILSs continue to retain a monopoly on software that's compatible with their own. Often, the only software compatible is that put out by the vendor who provides the ILS.
- Read the contract carefully, and determine who owns the usage data of the catalog, where it resides, and how you can use the information. For example, can you access your usage statistics immediately and extract information to analyze specific data, or do you have to request that information from your vendor? If so, can you use the information for in-house purposes as well as external (e.g., research and publications). While not an issue that we've had to consider in the past, this is becoming an increasingly important area to address.

Social catalogs may very well be the solution to libraries' attempts to extend the services of the library outside its physical walls into an online, socially connected community. The idea that we can connect our users to one another through books, movies, community events, or programs in a virtual environment is exciting and rewarding. While the potential that social catalogs have hasn't even begun to be explored fully, properly evaluating the new catalogs available to us and how we want to use the social technologies available in these catalogs should be explored prior to purchasing any catalog. If you firmly understand what you want today and are aware of what that software can do tomorrow, the entire process will go more smoothly and allow your library team to maintain strong objectives and benchmarks for assessing the success of the catalog. How do we want to connect our users? How does the library view its role in the online social environment? These are all big questions and require serious consideration. Although it's a big commitment, social catalogs may indeed become the primary interface for interaction with our communities, exceeding the use of our physical branches. So the last bit of advice for any those interested in social catalogs—expect challenges and rewards, but overall have fun! That's what social technology is all about.

Index